Kentucky Legal Research

Carolina Academic Press
Legal Research Series

Suzanne E. Rowe, Series Editor
Tenielle Fordyce-Ruff, Associate Series Editor

Arizona, Second Edition—Tamara S. Herrera

Arkansas, Second Edition—Coleen M. Barger, Cheryl L. Reinhart & Cathy L. Underwood

California, Third Edition—Aimee Dudovitz, Hether C. Macfarlane & Suzanne E. Rowe

Colorado—Robert Michael Linz

Connecticut—Jessica G. Hynes

Federal, Second Edition—Mary Garvey Algero, Spencer L. Simons, Suzanne E. Rowe, Scott Childs & Sarah E. Ricks

Florida, Fourth Edition—Barbara J. Busharis, Jennifer LaVia & Suzanne E. Rowe

Georgia—Nancy P. Johnson, Elizabeth G. Adelman & Nancy J. Adams

Idaho, Second Edition—Tenielle Fordyce-Ruff & Kristina J. Running

Illinois, Second Edition—Mark E. Wojcik

Iowa, Second Edition—John D. Edwards, Karen L. Wallace & Melissa H. Weresh

Kansas—Joseph A. Custer & Christopher L. Steadham

Kentucky, Second Edition—William A. Hilyerd, Kurt X. Metzmeier & David J. Ensign

Louisiana, Second Edition—Mary Garvey Algero

Massachusetts, Second Edition—E. Joan Blum & Shaun B. Spencer

Michigan, Third Edition—Cristina D. Lockwood & Pamela Lysaght

Minnesota—Suzanne Thorpe

Mississippi—Kristy L. Gilliland

Missouri, Third Edition—Wanda M. Temm & Julie M. Cheslik

New York, Third Edition—Elizabeth G. Adelman, Theodora Belniak Courtney L. Selby & Brian Detweiler

North Carolina, Second Edition—Scott Childs & Sara Sampson

North Dakota—Anne Mullins & Tammy Pettinato

Ohio, Second Edition—Sara Sampson, Katherine L. Hall & Carolyn Broering-Jacobs

Oklahoma—Darin K. Fox, Darla W. Jackson & Courtney L. Selby

Oregon, Third Edition Revised Printing—Suzanne E. Rowe

Pennsylvania—Barbara J. Busharis & Bonny L. Tavares

Tennessee, Second Edition—Scott Childs, Sibyl Marshall & Carol McCrehan Parker

Texas, Second Edition—Spencer L. Simons

Washington, Second Edition—Julie Heintz-Cho, Tom Cobb & Mary A. Hotchkiss

West Virginia—Hollee Schwartz Temple

Wisconsin—Patricia Cervenka & Leslie Behroozi

Wyoming, Second Edition—Debora A. Person & Tawnya K. Plumb

Kentucky Legal Research

SECOND EDITION

William A. Hilyerd
Kurt X. Metzmeier
David J. Ensign

Suzanne E. Rowe, Series Editor
Tenielle Fordyce-Ruff, Associate Series Editor

Carolina Academic Press
Durham, North Carolina

Library of Congress Cataloging-in-Publication Data

Names: Hilyerd, William A. author. | Metzmeier, Kurt X. author. | Ensign, David (David J.) author.
Title: Kentucky legal research / William A. Hilyerd, Kurt X. Metzmeier, and David J. Ensign.
Description: Second edition. | Durham, North Carolina : Carolina Academic Press, 2017. | Series: Legal Research Series | Includes bibliographical references and index.
Identifiers: LCCN 2017004885 | ISBN 9781611637076 (alk. paper)
Subjects: LCSH: Legal research--Kentucky.
Classification: LCC KFK1275 .H55 2017 | DDC 340.072/0769--dc23
LC record available at https://lccn.loc.gov/2017004885

Carolina Academic Press

700 Kent Street
Durham, North Carolina 27701
Telephone (919) 489-7486
Fax (919) 493-5668
www.cap-press.com

Printed in the United States of America.

Summary of Contents

Contents

List of Tables and Figures

Series Note

The Legal Research Series published by Carolina Academic Press includes titles from many states around the country as well as a separate text on federal legal research. The goal of each book is to provide law students, practitioners, paralegals, college students, laypeople, and librarians with the essential elements of legal research in each jurisdiction. Unlike more bibliographic texts, the Legal Research Series books seek to explain concisely both the sources of legal research and the process for conducting legal research effectively.

Preface

Kentucky Legal Research has been written to assist readers in acquiring and perfecting legal research skills. Since there are a wide range of options for locating primary and secondary materials, we include both print and electronic sources. Throughout the chapters, we refer to commercial providers of computerized legal research, primarily Lexis and Westlaw but also Casemaker, which is now free to members of the Kentucky Bar Association. We are also careful to discuss all relevant Internet websites maintained by the Kentucky government.

The text begins with an overview of the research process and legal analysis. The objectives of each chapter include an explanation of research strategies and a discussion of print and electronic resources. To simplify the research process, we often include detailed description of various research tasks. We also provide a variety of examples and screen shots to illustrate the sources. Some chapters include appendixes that provide the researcher with more detailed information.

Each chapter gives a very brief explanation of appropriate federal materials that could be used with Kentucky materials. Since legal ethics research is very important, a separate chapter addresses that topic. At the end of the book, there is an appendix briefly discussing Kentucky citation rules and a selective bibliography of legal research materials.

As explained in Appendix A, attorneys in Kentucky use citations that vary somewhat from the national formats. The ones that readers will encounter most frequently in this book are using "KRS" for the Kentucky Revised Statutes, "KAR" for the *Kentucky Administrative Regulations Service*, and "Com." to abbreviate the Commonwealth of Kentucky in case names.

Acknowledgments

Professor Suzanne E. Rowe, the series editor, greatly improved the quality of this book by reviewing each chapter. Moreover, as the author of previous books in this series, Professor Rowe shared freely from her own body of work. In this regard, the authors acknowledge, in particular, Professor Rowe's significant contributions to Chapters 1, 3, and 7.

The authors are grateful to Mike Swansburg, Benjamin I. Silver, Barbara Westerfield Hilyerd, Jamison McCune, Jennifer Reynolds, Rowen Hardenbrook, Ashley Wong, and Aleisha Cowles for reading and proofreading all or parts of the manuscript, and Beth Haendiges for drawing Table 11-2 and for proofreading Chapters 2, 5, 6, and 10.

The authors acknowledge LexisNexis and Thomson Reuters for granting permission to include images of their products and services. The authors also wish to acknowledge support for this work from the University of Louisville, Louis D. Brandeis School of Law.

Kentucky Legal Research

Chapter 1

The Research Process and Legal Analysis[1]

I. Kentucky Legal Research

The fundamentals of legal research are the same in every American jurisdiction, though the details vary. While some variations are minor, others require specialized knowledge of the resources available and the analytical framework in which those resources are used. This book focuses on the resources and analysis required to be thorough and effective in researching Kentucky law. It supplements this focus with brief explanations of federal research to introduce additional resources and to highlight some of the variations.

This book is not designed to be a blueprint of every resource in the law library or search engine on the Internet; many resources contain their own detailed explanations in a preface or a "help" section. This book is more like a manual or field guide, introducing the resources needed at each step of the research process, and explaining how to use them.

II. The Intersection of Legal Research and Legal Analysis

The basic process of legal research is simple. For most online research, you will search particular websites or databases using words likely to appear in the text of relevant documents. For most print resources, you begin with an index, find entries that appear relevant, read those sections of the text, and then find out whether more recent information is available.

Legal analysis is interwoven throughout this process, raising challenging questions. In print research, which words will you look up in the index? How will you decide whether an index entry looks promising? With online research, how will

1. Portions of this chapter were drawn from *Oregon Legal Research* by Suzanne E. Rowe and are used with permission.

you choose relevant words and construct a search most likely to produce the documents you need? When you read the text of a document, how will you determine whether it is relevant to your client's situation? How will you learn whether material that is more recent changed the law or merely applied it in a new situation? The answer to each of these questions requires legal analysis. This intersection of research and analysis can make legal research very difficult, especially for the novice. While this book's focus is legal research, it also includes the fundamental aspects of legal analysis required to conduct research competently.

III. Types of Legal Authority

Before researching the law, you must be clear about the goal of your search. In almost every research situation, you will want to find constitutional provisions, statutes, administrative rules, and judicial opinions that control your client's situation. In other words, you are searching for primary, mandatory authority.

Law is often divided along two lines. The first line distinguishes primary authority from secondary authority. *Primary authority* is law produced by governmental bodies with law-making power. Legislatures write statutes; courts write judicial opinions; and administrative agencies write rules, also called regulations. *Secondary authority* is commentary or analysis of the law, which may be written by attorneys, judges, law professors, or non-governmental bodies. Secondary authority includes sources such as law review articles, treatises, and legal encyclopedias. These secondary sources are designed to aid you in understanding the law and locating primary authority.

Another division is made between mandatory and persuasive authority. *Mandatory authority* is binding on the court that would decide a conflict if the situation were litigated. In a question of Kentucky law, mandatory authority includes the Kentucky constitution, statutes enacted by the Kentucky legislature, opinions of the Kentucky Supreme Court, and Kentucky administrative regulations. Opinions of the Kentucky Court of Appeals are binding on district courts and circuit courts.

Persuasive authority is not binding, but may be followed by a court if relevant and well reasoned. Persuasive authority includes sources such as court cases from other states that are on point, relevant statutes from other states, or the opinions of legal experts expressed in law review articles or treatises. Persuasive authority might be particularly helpful when the mandatory authority in Kentucky is contrary to your client's position, and you want to persuade a court to change current precedential authority, or when the case is one of first impression. While primary authority may be used as mandatory or persuasive authority, secondary authority is always only persuasive if on point.

Table 1-1. Overview of the Research Process

1. Gather facts, decide which jurisdiction controls, and *generate a list of research terms.*
2. Consult *secondary authorities* such as practice guides, treatises, legal encyclopedias, and law review articles. Secondary authorities explain the law and refer to primary authorities.
3. Find controlling *constitutional provisions, statutes,* or *rules* by reviewing their indexes or searching online for your research terms. Read these primary authorities carefully, update them if necessary, and then study their annotations for cross-references to additional authorities and explanatory materials.
4. Find citations to *cases* by searching *digests* or *online databases.* A digest is essentially a multi-volume topic index of cases in a certain jurisdiction or subject area.
5. Read the cases either in *reporters* or *online.* A reporter series publishes the full text of cases in a certain jurisdiction or subject area.
6. *Update* legal authorities by using a citator such as Shepard's or KeyCite to (a) ensure that an authority is still respected and (b) find additional sources that may be relevant to the research project.
7. *End* your research when you have no holes in your analysis and when you begin seeing the same authorities repeatedly.

Within primary, mandatory authority there is an interlocking hierarchy of law involving constitutions, statutes, administrative rules, and judicial opinions. The constitution of each state is the supreme law of that state. If a statute is on point, that statute comes next in the hierarchy, followed by administrative rules. Judicial opinions may interpret the statute or rule, but they cannot disregard it. A judicial opinion may decide that a statute violates the constitution or that a rule oversteps its bounds. If there is no constitutional provision, statute or administrative rule on point, *common law,* also called judge-made law, may control the issue.

IV. Overview of the Research Process

Conducting effective legal research means following a process. The process leads to authority that controls a legal issue as well as to commentary that may help you analyze new and complex legal matters. The outline in Table 1-1 presents the basic research process.

The basic process should be customized for each research project. Consider whether you need to follow all seven steps, and if so, in what order. If you are unfamiliar with an area of law, you should follow each step of the process in the order indicated. Beginning with secondary sources will provide both context for the issues you must research and citations to relevant primary authority. As you gain experience in researching legal questions, you may choose to modify the process. For example, if you know that a situation is controlled by a statute, you may choose to begin with that step.

A. Getting Started

1. Gathering Facts and Determining Jurisdiction

The first step in any research project is to be sure you have a clear understanding of the problem. You should gather the facts of the client's situation to understand what is within the subject matter of the issue to be researched. It may be just as important to understand what is *not* included in the research project. You should understand the desired outcome of the research project. Is this a limited project on which you are to spend little time, or is this an extensive project such as an appellate brief, requiring exhaustive research and much time?

An early question that arises for any research project is which jurisdiction's law controls. This book assumes that the client's situation is controlled by Kentucky law, but you must determine whether federal law, the law of another state, or local law is binding. By determining the jurisdiction at an early stage of the project, you can identify sources that you will need to use and eliminate the need for others.

2. Generating Research Terms

After gathering facts and determining jurisdiction, generate a list of research terms. Many legal resources in print use lengthy indexes as the starting point for finding legal authority. Electronic sources often require the researcher to enter words that are likely to appear in a synopsis or in the full text of relevant documents. To ensure you are thorough in beginning a research project, you will need a comprehensive list of words, terms, and phrases that may lead to law on point. These may be legal terms or common words that describe the client's situation. The items on this list are research terms.

Organized brainstorming is the best way to compile a comprehensive list of research terms. Consider the things involved in your set of facts. What legal action might be filed and what defenses are possible? What relief is the

Table 1-2. Generating Research Terms

TARP Approach	
Things:	Dog, pit bull
Action:	Liability
Relief:	Damages, medical expenses, lost wages
Parties:	Paper girl, newspaper carrier, home owner, dog owner
Journalistic Approach	
Who:	Newspaper carrier, paper girl, invitee
What:	Liability, damages for injury
How:	Dog bite, pit bull
Why:	Lost wages, medical expenses
When:	Morning
Where:	Dog owner's yard

plaintiff seeking? Who are the parties involved in the action?[2] Brainstorming by asking these questions is sometimes referred to by the mnemonic TARP, which stands for things, action, relief, and parties. Another approach to generating research terms is to ask the journalistic questions: Who? What? How? Why? When? Where?

When generating your list of terms, try to think of synonyms. Also keep in mind the hierarchical arrangement of the law related to your problem. It may be necessary to consult more general or more specific terms when researching the problem. Some resources might list *libel* as a separate entry in an index, while others might list it as a sub-heading under *defamation*. As your research progresses, you may want to add words and phrases to your list of research terms, or you may take others off.

As an example, assume your client, a newspaper carrier, was bitten by a customer's pit bull while attempting to deliver the customer's newspaper. She is suing the owner of the dog to recover lost wages and medical expenses. You have been asked to research the liability of dog owners for injuries caused to others. Table 1-2 lists possible research terms, using the approaches discussed above.

2. *See* C. Edward Good, *Legal Research ... Without Losing Your Mind* 61–62 (LEL Enterprises 1993).

B. Choosing to Research in Print or Online

Much information, especially that in secondary sources, can be found only in print. However, many resources are available both in print and online. A comprehensive research strategy often includes information found in both media. When deciding which medium to use, consider the following:

- How authoritative is the information? Be sure that the source of your information is reputable and not biased.
- How current is the information? Pocket parts[3] and supplements may require much time to be printed and distributed, making information in them less current than an online counterpart. Print publications can be discontinued, or subscriptions may lapse. Be sure to note the copyright date or the publication date on the most recent supplement. Even in online research, be sure that the page you are reviewing has current information.
- Is the information retrospective? Online sources sometimes include only recent material and may not cover the time period required for the research project.
- How much does an online search cost, and who is paying? Some online sites are free to search, while some commercial services can be very expensive. The cost may be worthwhile if an accurate and efficient search is conducted.
- How fast and efficient will the search be? Sometimes online searches are faster and more efficient than print research. It is a mistake to assume that this is always the case, however. Often, the same information can be found more easily and quickly in a print source.
- How much context is provided? Print sources sometimes provide better hierarchical or organizational context than online sources. This context, together with editorial features such as cross-references to related topics, can result in more complete and accurate research.

V. Researching the Law—Organization of This Book

The remainder of this book explains how to conduct legal research in a variety of sources. Although the research process often begins with secondary

3. Pocket parts are additional pages inserted in a slot in the back cover of books, providing updated information.

sources, the book begins with primary authority because that authority is the goal of legal research. Chapters 3 and 4 explain how to research judicial decisions. Chapters 2, 5, and 6 describe the Kentucky constitution, statutory law, and legislative history research, respectively. Chapter 7 addresses administrative law, and Chapter 8 discusses researching court rules and professional ethics.

After this focus on primary authority, the following chapters explain how to update legal authority using KeyCite and Shepard's citators (Chapter 9) and how to use secondary sources and practice aids (Chapter 10). Although each chapter includes relevant website addresses for online research and many chapters discuss online search techniques, Chapter 11 provides additional information for conducting legal research online.

Appendix A provides an overview of the conventions lawyers follow in citing legal authority in their documents. Appendix B contains a selected bibliography of texts on legal research and analysis. The general research texts tend to concentrate on federal resources, supplementing this book's brief introduction to those resources.

Chapter 2

The Kentucky Constitution

Can a national grocery store pay its employees in food?[1] If your shift at work lasts the entire time the polls are open, does your employer have to give you time to vote?[2] If the owner of a riverboat decides to give Louisville's mayor a free pass to honor his efforts to promote the city's riverfront, can he take it?[3] Answers to all of these legal questions can be traced not to the Kentucky statutes or to the decisions of Kentucky courts, but to the commonwealth's singularly inclusive constitution. They illustrate the importance of including the state constitution as part of any serious legal research project.

The current Constitution of the Commonwealth of Kentucky is the state's fourth charter. It was debated and drafted in a constitutional convention that met throughout 1890 and 1891 and was ratified in 1891. The document is wide-ranging, often touching on areas not usually the subject of state constitutions. Thus, as a responsible legal researcher, you should always check whether or not the subject of your inquiry is governed by a constitutional provision very early on in your research, acting on the assumption that just about any topic can be found in Kentucky's constitution. Moreover, such research might suggest interesting arguments that may not be otherwise apparent. If a provision does apply, you should then examine its legislative history and the judicial decisions interpreting it.

---

1. No. "All wage-earners in this State employed in factories, mines, workshops, or by corporations, shall be paid for their labor in lawful money." Ky. Const. § 244.

2. Yes. "The General Assembly shall provide by law that all employers shall allow employees, under reasonable regulations, at least four hours on election days, in which to cast their votes." Ky. Const. § 148.

3. No. "No railroad, steamboat or other common carrier, under heavy penalty to be fixed by the General Assembly, shall give a free pass or passes, or shall, at reduced rates not common to the public, sell tickets for transportation to any State, district, city, town or county officer." Ky. Const. § 197.

Table 2-1. Outline of the Kentucky Constitution

- Bill of rights (§§ 1–26)
- State government, generally (§§ 27–28)
- Legislative branch (§§ 29–62)
- Impeachments (§§ 66–68)
- Executive branch (§§ 69–108)
- Judicial branch (§§ 109–139)
- County government (§§ 63–65, 140–144)
- Suffrage and elections (§§ 145–155)
- Municipal government (§§ 156–168)
- Revenue and taxation (§§ 169–182)
- Education (§§ 183–189)
- Corporations (§§ 190–208)
- Railroads and commerce (§§ 209–218)
- State militia (§§ 219–223)
- General provisions (§§ 224–255) including lotteries (§ 226), sovereign immunity (§ 231), dueling (§§ 239–240), wrongful death (§ 241), and juries (§ 248)
- Revising the constitution (§§ 256–263)

In recent years, state courts have found that their state's bill of rights and constitution can provide independent and, in some cases, greater protection of individual rights. Such thinking, for example, caused the Kentucky Supreme Court to find that a law criminalizing consensual sodomy was inconsistent with the personal liberties guaranteed by the state bill of rights more than a decade before the U.S. Supreme Court found such rights in the federal Constitution.[4] When the federal courts' reading of individual liberties narrows, smart attorneys now comb the state constitution to find support for their case.

The Kentucky constitution begins with a bill of rights that has some important variations from the federal version. Following this are sections outlining Kentucky's state and local government, various provisions on specific matters ranging from education to dueling, and mechanisms for revising the constitution. Table 2-1 outlines the sections of the Kentucky constitution.

4. *Com. v. Wasson*, 842 S.W.2d 487 (Ky. 1992).

I. Researching the Kentucky Constitution

A. The Constitution in *Michie's Kentucky Revised Statutes* and *Baldwin's Kentucky Revised Statutes*

The Kentucky legislature has mandated that the Kentucky constitution be included in all official versions of the state statutory code, the Kentucky Revised Statutes (KRS). This means the best places to find cases interpreting constitutional provisions are Kentucky's two annotated codes. Both *Michie's Kentucky Revised Statutes* and *Baldwin's Kentucky Revised Statutes* include fully annotated versions of the current constitution. The *Michie's Kentucky Revised Statutes* volume containing the state constitution includes unannotated versions of the three prior state constitutions and a very helpful index. Kentucky's constitution is spread over the first two volumes of *Baldwin's Kentucky Revised Statutes*, and a detailed index can be found at the end of the second volume. The two official codes annotate each provision of the constitution with cross-references to the Kentucky Revised Statutes, judicial decisions of federal and Kentucky courts, law review and bar journal articles, legal treatises, and published opinions of the Kentucky Attorney General.

B. The Constitution on Lexis and Westlaw

Lexis has designated a separate database for the constitution volume of its Michie's KRS, but to find it you need to pick Kentucky from the "State" tab of "Explore Content" and scroll down to "Statutes & Legislation." From there you can click "Kentucky Constitution" to search the entire document or click the table of contents icon to browse it by section.

The state constitution is also available in the annotated KRS found on Westlaw. Under "Browse," choose "State Materials," then "Kentucky." From there, click "Kentucky Statutes & Court Rules" to bring up a table of contents version which you can browse or search. From this page you can use a few useful commands. To view a document with a known citation, you can use **ky const s [number]**. For example, use **ky const s 1** to retrieve the first section of the constitution. Also, to find what the constitution says about common carriers (or any other topic), you might use the search **ci(ky const) & "common carrier."** Another useful feature is that you can, from the table of contents page, choose to search the 1792, 1799, and 1850 Kentucky constitutions.

C. Free Online Sources for the Kentucky Constitution

While some rudimentary Internet legal research on the state constitution is possible, it is perhaps best to look at web resources as supplementing print research. A full-text, searchable version of the current constitution is available on the Kentucky legislature's website (http://www.lrc.ky.gov). This version can be browsed by section title and number or searched by the website's simple search engine. Note, however, that some searches may bring misleading results. For example, a search of **gambling** returns no hits. This is because the constitution refers to "lotteries," not gambling, and there are no annotations to supplement the bare text of the document in searching for that term. The legislature has also issued the state charter in book form, *The Constitution of the Commonwealth of Kentucky* (Kentucky Legislative Research Commission 2015) which can be requested in print from lrcpublications@lrc.ky.gov or downloaded (http://www.lrc.ky.gov/lrcpubs/IB59.pdf).

The two official versions of the Kentucky Revised Statutes have versions of Kentucky's prior three constitutions as well as the original text of the current 1891 constitution. The Kentucky State Law Library scanned the debates of the convention that drafted the 1890–91 constitution and worked with the University of Louisville Law Library to place them online. The University of Louisville Law Library has already digitized the debates and records of the convention that promulgated the 1850 constitution and has published them as part of the University of Louisville's Digital Library Collection (http://digital.library.louisville.edu/cdm/landingpage/collection/law). While there are no debates for the 1792 and 1799 constitutions, the University of Kentucky Law Library has published the journals online (http://uknowledge.uky.edu/ky_cons_conventions/).

D. Commentaries

One of the best guides to the state constitution is the regularly updated *Citizens' Guide to the Kentucky Constitution* (Kentucky Legislative Research Commission 2013), published by the state legislature. This publication, which is available online (http://www.lrc.ky.gov/lrcpubs/RR137.pdf) and can be sent free of cost on request, summarizes the content, history, and judicial treatment of major sections of the constitution. There are tables of amendments and an excellent index that covers both the main text and the appendices.

Robert M. Ireland's *The Kentucky State Constitution: A Reference Guide* (Oxford 2011) is also an important resource. Ireland, Kentucky's foremost legal historian, details the historical background and legal development of the state's 1891 constitution, with detailed commentary on every section of the document.

II. Interpreting the Kentucky Constitution

The interpretation of the state constitution by Kentucky's appellate courts follows three lines. First, in some cases, courts attempt to analyze the language of the document. Second, courts will look at the historical context in which the provision was drafted, with a particular interest in the printed debates and records of constitutional conventions (or the legislature in the case of amendments). Third, judicial decisions of prior courts are examined, with a particular interest in decisions rendered soon after the adoption of the constitution. (This is based on the theory that those early decisions were decided by judges who likely participated in the activities leading to the adoption of the constitution and thus were more likely to understand the meaning of its language.)

A good example of how the Kentucky courts go about analyzing a constitutional issue is the case of *Commonwealth v. Wasson*[5] where the Kentucky Supreme Court invalidated the state's law criminalizing consensual sodomy on the grounds that it violated the appellant's right to privacy and to the equal protection of the law under Sections 1, 2, and 3 of the Kentucky constitution.

The Kentucky Supreme Court began its analysis by clearly establishing its independent right to find protections for individual rights in the state charter "so long as state constitutional protection does not fall below the federal *floor*" set by the United States Supreme Court.[6] This was important because the issues raised could also be argued under the U.S. Constitution and the federal courts have found that state courts must clearly find that a "non-federal ground independently and adequately supports the judgment."[7]

The court then quoted from the debates of the convention, in an attempt to determine the intent of the drafters of the relevant provisions. The court then examined a decision rendered just after the constitution was adopted which, in the context of home use of prohibited liquor, said that it was "not within the competency of government to invade the privacy of a citizen's life and to regulate his conduct in matters in which he alone is concerned."[8] The

---

5. *Id.*
6. *Id.* at 492.
7. *Michigan v. Long*, 463 U.S. 1032, 1038 (1983).
8. *Com. v. Campbell*, 117 S.W. 383, 385 (Ky. 1909).

court was persuaded that a case which had been decided by a judge who had lived at the time of adoption of the state constitution was a good guide to the meaning of that document.

A. Text

When a judge is tasked with interpreting any document, including a constitutional provision, his or her first instinct is to apply the standard tools of construction. But, as the court in *Varney v. Justice* noted in 1888, a state constitution is very different from a statute.[9] Unlike a statute, which can be corrected at the next session, a constitution is meant to be permanent and thus courts should "construe a Constitution with great caution" and should "not give it a technical construction which will defeat it."[10]

Kentucky's courts have found that the "meaning of a word or a phrase," in the state constitution, "is not to be determined by the dictionary alone, for its context and association may often be controlling"[11] and advised that the constitution "is concerned with substance and not with form and its framers did not intend to forbid a common-sense application of its provisions."[12] In general, courts have found that "the constitution should be construed liberally," and "[d]oubtful questions ought to be resolved in favor of the freedom of the living generation to govern its own affairs in the light of modern circumstances."[13]

Nonetheless, Kentucky judicial decisions have offered a few tools of linguistic analysis. First, courts have noted that in "construing one section of a Constitution [the] court should not isolate it from other sections, but all the sections bearing on any particular subject should be brought into consideration and be so interpreted as to effectuate the whole purpose of the Constitution."[14] Moreover, different sections of the constitution concerning the same subject, "but making different provisions concerning them should be read together and construed so as to reconcile the provisions."[15] Finally, where the constitu-

9. *Varney v. Justice*, 6 S.W. 457, 459 (Ky. 1888).

10. *Herold v. Talbott*, 88 S.W.2d 303, 305 (Ky. 1935).

11. *Jefferson Cnty. ex rel. Grauman v. Jefferson Cnty. Fiscal Ct.*, 117 S.W.2d 918, 921 (Ky. 1938).

12. *Keck v. Manning*, 231 S.W.2d 604, 607 (Ky. 1950), following *Meredith v. Kauffman*, 169 S.W.2d 37, 39 (Ky. 1943).

13. *Board of Educ. of Graves Cnty. v. De Weese*, 343 S.W.2d 598, 606 (Ky. 1960).

14. *Grantz v. Grauman*, 302 S.W.2d 364, 366 (Ky. 1957) (adopting language of 11 Am. Jur. *Constitutional Law* § 53, p. 661).

15. *Pinkston v. Watkins*, 216 S.W. 852, 854 (Ky. 1919).

tion's "language used is prohibitory, it was intended to be a positive and unequivocal negation," and, "[w]henever the language contains a grant of power, it was intended as a mandate."[16]

B. Case Law

In addition to analyzing the language of a constitutional provision, it is obviously important to look at cases that have interpreted that section. As previously noted, Kentucky courts have announced a preference for the "principle of contemporaneous construction," which holds that "cases decided contemporaneously or close in time" to the adoption of the state constitution "are entitled to greater weight in our constitutional analysis."[17] The theory is based on the idea that the judges on courts sitting in recent memory of the adoption of a constitution (some of which may have served as delegates to the Kentucky constitutional convention), "wrote with a direct, firsthand knowledge of the mind set of [the] constitutional fathers."[18]

C. Researching Historical Circumstances

In determining the proper construction to give to the language in the state constitution, Kentucky courts "must look to the history of the times and the state of existing things to ascertain the intention of the framers of the Constitution and the people adopting it, and a practical interpretation will be given to the end that the plainly manifested purpose of those who created the Constitution, or its amendments, may be carried out."[19] Kentucky's high court has said that while "the Constitution is not static, but progressive, in its application to meet changed conditions," the "meaning of a constitutional provision never varies."[20]

Kentucky's courts have found that the surest tool of historical analysis is the published debates of the conventions that introduced the language provisions into the current charter. The most important document is the records and debates of the 1890–1891 convention. However, as that convention took as its starting point the state's three prior constitutions, adopting much of the older language without much comment, evidence of the intentions of the adopters

---

16. *Varney*, 6 S.W. at 459.
17. *Williams v. Wilson*, 972 S.W.2d 260, 267 (Ky. 1998).
18. *Id.* (quoting *Com. v. Wasson*, 842 S.W.2d 487, 492 (Ky. 1992)).
19. *Eaton Asphalt Paving Co. v. CSX Transp., Inc.*, 8 S.W.3d 878, 882 (Ky. App. 1999) (quoting *Keck v. Manning*, 231 S.W.2d 604, 607 (Ky. 1950)).
20. *Herold*, 88 S.W.2d at 305.

of that earlier language has also been examined by courts. Unfortunately, of Kentucky's three other constitutional conventions, only the delegates that assembled in 1849–1850 saw fit to publish their debates in full. Since many provisions, especially the state bill of rights, date back to the first constitution, courts interpreting them have had to turn to secondary sources and other state constitutions with related histories.

1. The 1891 Constitutional Convention

Any detailed research into a provision of the current Kentucky constitution must inevitably include inquiry into the intentions of the Constitutional Convention of 1890–1891. The debates of this body are printed in the four, thick volumes of the *Official Report of the Proceedings and Debates in the Convention Assembled at Frankfort, on the Eighth Day of September, 1890, to Adapt, Amend, or Change the Constitution of the State of Kentucky* (1891). The *Proceedings and Debates* is a chronological, verbatim transcript of the debates of the convention. One problem with the set is that the index is poorly designed, with overly broad headings and too strong a focus on the name of the speaker, instead of what was said. The Legislative Research Commission remedied the problem somewhat with its 1989 publication, *Index to the Debates of the 1890 Constitutional Convention*, although this title is out of print and somewhat difficult to find. As noted above, the State Law Library and the University of Louisville have placed a version on the University of Louisville Law Library Digital Collection (http://digital.library.louisville.edu/cdm/landingpage/collection/law/).

There is also an excellent secondary source that provides detailed analysis and historical commentary on each section of the state constitution, Robert M. Ireland's *The Kentucky State Constitution: A Reference Guide.*

2. Prior Constitutions

Many provisions of the Kentucky constitution have been held over from the state's earlier charters. For example, the state bill of rights is largely derived from its initial 1792 constitution. In many cases, the delegates of the 1890–1891 constitutional convention accepted these older provisions into the state constitution without extended comment. In such situations, researchers have to look back beyond 1891 to find historical intent.

a. The 1849 Constitution

The Constitutional Convention of 1849 was the first convention to publish its debates and records. The one-volume *Report of the Debates and Proceedings of the Convention for the Revision of the Constitution of the State of Kentucky*

(1849) made it possible for citizens voting on the measure to know the intentions of the delegates. The *Debates and Proceedings* are available online as part of the University of Louisville Law Library Digital Collection (http://digital.library.louisville.edu/cdm/landingpage/collection/law/).

b. The 1792 and 1799 Constitutions

The documentary history of the 1792 and 1799 conventions is slight. In 1942, the state bar association published the brief journal of the 1792 convention on its sesquicentennial.[21] This document did not include minutes of the debates. Since much of the 1792 constitution is based on the 1790 Pennsylvania constitution, the documentary history of that document is useful. Fortunately, an electronic version of the published debates of the 1790 constitutional convention is available free at Duquesne University School of Law's Pennsylvania Constitution website (http://www.duq.edu/academics/gumberg-library/pa-constitution). The daily journal of the 1799 Kentucky constitutional convention is only available on microfilm and is a short, bare outline of each day's activities. It contains no debates or records, except some correspondence from the papers of the governor. As noted above, digital versions of the journals of the 1792 and 1799 conventions are available from the University of Kentucky (http://uknowledge.uky.edu/ky_cons_conventions/).

There are two good histories of the 1792 constitution that may assist researchers: Joan Wells Coward's *Kentucky in the New Republic: The Process of Constitution Making* (University Press of Kentucky 1979) and Lowell H. Harrison's *Kentucky's Road to Statehood* (University Press of Kentucky 1992). Coward's *Kentucky in the New Republic* also has the best account of the 1799 constitutional convention and its political context.

3. Post-1891 Amendments

Several notable amendments to the 1891 constitution have been adopted over the last hundred years, from changes to allow reform of the judicial system to the provision for a state-run lottery. A table of these amendments can be found in an appendix to the *Citizens' Guide to the Kentucky Constitution*.

To research a recently amended section of the 1891 constitution, first carefully examine the official annotated Kentucky Revised Statutes. Take care to note any annotations to law review and bar journal articles; they may have been written by persons involved in drafting or implementing the amendment.

---

21. *Journal of the First Constitutional Convention of Kentucky, Held in Danville, Kentucky, April 2 to 19, 1792* (State Bar Assoc. of Kentucky 1942).

Research the documentary history of the amendment in the same way that you would trace the legislative history of statutes. First, check the official annotated KRS to determine the citation to the volume of the *Kentucky Acts* where the provision was first proposed. Read that act and look for the House or Senate bill number it had as it passed through the General Assembly. With that number, you can use tables in the House and Senate journals to track the amendment from its first reading to its final passage. (For more on legislative history, see Chapter 6.)

After an amendment passes out of the legislature, it is placed on the ballot and faces the verdict of the voters. The state board of elections, as custodian of the official election results, has records of the voting results for all constitutional amendments back to 1973 on its website (http://elect.ky.gov/). In researching amendments enacted since 1967, you should not ignore the documents of the Constitutional Revision Assembly because some provisions under the failed 1966 constitution have been passed as separate amendments. *The Final Report of the Constitutional Revision Assembly*, published in 1966 by the Legislative Research Commission, is a key document.

There are secondary sources that you can also use to help interpret significant amendments. First, Robert M. Ireland's *The Kentucky State Constitution: A Reference Guide* has at least something for each provision. The 1975 amendment reforming the entire judicial article is described in Kurt X. Metzmeier, Michael Whiteman and Jason Nemes, *United at Last: The Judicial Article and the Struggle to Reform Kentucky's Courts* (Court of Justice 2006).

III. Researching Other State Constitutions with Similar Provisions

In areas where the Kentucky constitution has not been extensively reviewed in published decisions of its state courts of appeal, researching constitutions from other states with similar constitutional provisions can be useful. While there is no perfect method for doing this, there are some useful resources to assist you.

In 1915, the New York State Constitutional Convention Commission commissioned Columbia University to research and to index all state constitutions as they existed at that time. The result was the *Index-Digest of State Constitutions*. After that project, Columbia continued the index with updates and a new second edition in 1959. In 1980, the project was reborn as a looseleaf set with full text of the constitutions, with the index-digest as the last volume, *Constitutions of the United States: National and State* (Oceana 1980). The index-digest will direct you to citations to similar sections in constitutions from other American states.

Oxford University Press, which has republished Robert M. Ireland's *The Kentucky State Constitution,* has reference guides for most other states. There are two inexpensive ways to obtain access to the text of all the state constitutions. One is to obtain a copy of the relatively inexpensive *State Constitutions of the United States* (Congressional Quarterly 2006). Another way is to check the state website of every state—nearly all have versions available.

IV. United States Constitution

The federal constitution is published along with the Kentucky constitution in *Michie's Kentucky Revised Statutes* and *Baldwin's Kentucky Revised Statutes.* It is also available in print in the first few volumes of *United States Code Annotated* and *United States Code Service.* An annotated version of the Constitution with commentary entitled *Constitution of the United States, Analysis and Interpretation* is maintained by the Congressional Research Service and is available at Congress.gov (https://www.congress.gov/constitution-annotated) and also on the U.S. Government Publishing Office's govinfo.gov website (https://www.govinfo.gov/collection/constitution-annotated). Annotated versions of the federal Constitution are also available on Lexis and Westlaw.

Chapter 3

Judicial Opinions and Reporters

A judicial opinion, also called a case, is written by a court to explain its decision in a particular dispute. Cases are published in rough chronological order in books called *reporters*. Some reporters include cases from courts within a specific geographic region. Other reporters include only cases decided by a certain court. For example, the *South Western Reporter* publishes state decisions for a group of states that includes Kentucky, while the *United States Reports* publishes only opinions issued by the United States Supreme Court. Still other reporters publish only those cases that deal with a certain topic, such as bankruptcy or tax.

This chapter outlines Kentucky and federal court systems, describes the various reporters and databases that contain the opinions of the courts in those systems, and offers strategies for reading and analyzing cases.

I. Court Systems

Because legal research includes reading judicial opinions, researchers need to understand the court system. The basic court structure includes trial courts, intermediate courts of appeal, and an ultimate appellate court, often called the "supreme" court. These courts exist at both state and federal levels.

A. Kentucky Courts

Currently, there are four levels of courts within the Kentucky judicial system. District courts are trial level courts of limited jurisdiction that can hear criminal misdemeanors, civil matters involving an amount in controversy of $5,000 or less, and uncontested probate matters.

Matters that originate in district court can be appealed to circuit courts. In addition, circuit courts act as trial level courts for all matters that do not fall within the limited jurisdiction of district courts, including criminal felonies and civil matters involving an amount in controversy exceeding $5,000.

Figure 3-1. Kentucky Court System

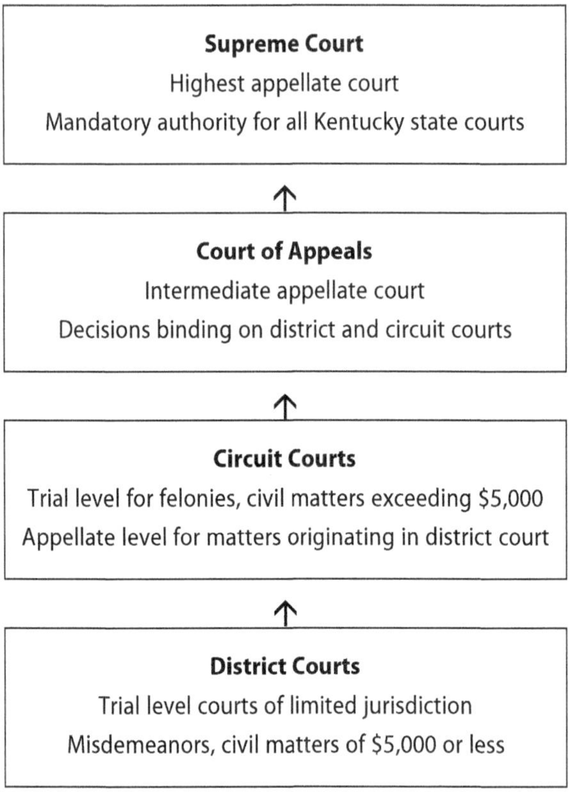

Issues appealed from the circuit courts are heard by three-judge panels in the Court of Appeals, which is Kentucky's intermediate appellate level. Final appeals are heard by the Kentucky Supreme Court.

The current court structure was established as a result of the judicial reform that took effect on January 1, 1976. Before that date, the Court of Appeals was designated as the state's court of last resort. Figure 3-1 illustrates the Kentucky court structure.

B. Federal Courts

In the federal judicial system, the trial courts are called United States District Courts. There are 94 district courts in the federal system, with each district drawn from a particular state. For the state of Kentucky, there are two districts: the Eastern District and the Western District.

Intermediate appellate courts in the federal system are called United States Courts of Appeals. There are courts of appeals for each of the thirteen federal circuits. Twelve of these circuits are based on geographic jurisdiction. Eleven numbered circuits cover all the states; the twelfth is the District of Columbia Circuit. The thirteenth federal circuit, called the Federal Circuit, hears appeals from district courts in all other circuits on issues related to patent law and from certain specialized courts and agencies. A map showing the federal circuits is available at the United States court's website (http://www.uscourts.gov/sites/default/files/u.s._federal_courts_circuit_map_1.pdf).

Kentucky is in the Sixth Circuit. This means that cases from the United States District Court for the two districts of Kentucky are appealed to the United States Court of Appeals for the Sixth Circuit. In addition to Kentucky, this circuit encompasses Michigan, Ohio, and Tennessee.

The highest court in the federal system is the United States Supreme Court. It decides cases concerning the United States Constitution and federal statutes. This Court does not have the final say on matters of purely state law; that authority rests with the highest court of each state. Parties who wish to have the U.S. Supreme Court hear their cases must file a petition for *certiorari*, as the Court has discretion over which cases it hears.

The website for the federal judiciary (http://www.uscourts.gov) contains maps, court addresses, explanations of jurisdictions, and other helpful information. The Supreme Court also has a useful website (http://www.supremecourt.gov).

C. Courts of Other States

Most states have a three-tier court system similar to that of the federal judiciary. Like Kentucky, a few do not. Some do not have an intermediate appellate court, just as Kentucky did not until the Judicial Reform of 1975. Another difference in some court systems is that the "supreme" court is not the highest court. In New York, the trial courts are called supreme courts and the highest court is the Court of Appeals. Two other states, Massachusetts and Maine, call their highest courts the Supreme Judicial Court.

Each jurisdiction maintains a website which describes its court structure, and includes links to other information such as reported decisions, dockets, forms, and court rules. Citation manuals are good references for learning the names and hierarchy of the courts, as well as for learning proper citation to legal authorities. The two most popular are the *ALWD Guide to Legal Citation*, written by Coleen M. Barger and the Association of Legal Writing

Directors,[1] and *The Bluebook: A Uniform System of Citation*,[2] written by students from several law schools. Appendix 1 of the *ALWD Guide* and Table T1 of the *Bluebook* provide information on federal and state courts.

II. Reporters for Kentucky Cases

Currently, those cases decided by the Kentucky Supreme Court and the Kentucky Court of Appeals that are published appear in the *South Western Reporter*. From 1785 through 1886, decisions of the Kentucky Court of Appeals, then the court of last resort, were published in *Kentucky Reports*. Beginning in 1886, Court of Appeals decisions appeared both in *Kentucky Reports* and in the *South Western Reporter*. *Kentucky Reports* ceased publication in 1951, and since then the *South Western Reporter* has been the official reporter of Kentucky decisions.

Early Kentucky decisions were first published in *nominative reporters* that were named for the person who compiled the cases. These nominative reporters were later incorporated into *Kentucky Reports* and assigned consecutive volume numbers within that set. Because citations to those early cases still include references to the nominative volumes, it is worth noting the names of the reporters and the volumes of *Kentucky Reports* in which their works appear. Table 3-1 converts Kentucky nominatives to *Kentucky Reports* citations.[3]

Cases from district courts and circuit courts in Kentucky are not published; in fact, few states publish opinions at the trial court level. Records of proceedings in those courts may be obtained directly from the clerk of court.

Commercial, regional reporters such as the *South Western Reporter* often publish opinions from courts of several states under a single title. The *South Western Reporter* publishes cases from the courts of the following states: Texas, Arkansas, Tennessee, Kentucky, and Missouri. The *South Western Reporter* includes cases from the intermediate and highest appellate courts of these states. Other regional reporters are *Atlantic Reporter*, *North Eastern Reporter*, *North Western Reporter*, *Pacific Reporter*, *South Eastern Reporter*, and *Southern Reporter*. The states whose cases are included in each of these regional reporters are listed in Table 3-2.

---

1. ALWD & Coleen M. Barger, *ALWD Guide to Legal Citation* (5th ed., Wolters Kluwer Law & Business 2014) ("*ALWD Guide*").

2. *The Bluebook: A Uniform System of Citation* (The Columbia Law Review et al. eds., 20th ed., The Harvard Law Review Ass'n 2015) ("*Bluebook*").

3. *Id.* at Table T1.

Table 3-1. Kentucky Nominative Reporters

Hughes	1785–1801	1 Ky. (Hughes)
Sneed	1801–1805	2 Ky. (Sneed)
Hardin	1805–1808	3 Ky. (Hard.)
Bibb	1808–1817	e.g., 4 Ky. (1 Bibb)
Marshall, A.K.	1817–1821	e.g., 8 Ky. (1 A.K. Marshall)
Littell's Selected Cases	1795–1821	e.g., 16 Ky. (1 Litt. Sel. Cas.)
Littell	1822–1824	e.g., 11 Ky. (1 Litt.)
Monroe, T.B.	1824–1828	e.g., 17 Ky. (1 T.B. Mon.)
Marshall, J.J.	1829–1832	e.g., 24 Ky. (1 J.J. Marsh.)
Dana	1833–1840	e.g., 31 Ky. (1 Dana)
Monroe, Ben	1840–1857	e.g., 40 Ky. (1 B. Mon.)
Metcalf	1858–1863	e.g., 58 Ky. (1 Met.)
Duvall	1863–1866	e.g., 62 Ky. (1 Duv.)
Bush	1866–1879	e.g., 64 Ky. (1 Bush)

Table 3-2. Regional Reporters and States Included

Atlantic Reporter (A., A.2d, A.3d)	Connecticut, Delaware, District of Columbia, Maine, Maryland, New Hampshire, New Jersey, Pennsylvania, Rhode Island, Vermont
North Eastern Reporter (N.E., N.E.2d, N.E.3d)	Illinois, Indiana, Massachusetts, New York, Ohio
North Western Reporter (N.W., N.W.2d)	Iowa, Michigan, Minnesota, Nebraska, North Dakota, South Dakota, Wisconsin
Pacific Reporter (P., P.2d, P.3d)	Alaska, Arizona, California, Colorado, Hawaii, Idaho, Kansas, Montana, Nevada, New Mexico, Oklahoma, Oregon, Utah, Washington, Wyoming
South Eastern Reporter (S.E., S.E.2d)	Georgia, North Carolina, South Carolina, Virginia, West Virginia
South Western Reporter (S.W., S.W.2d, S.W.3d)	Arkansas, Kentucky, Missouri, Tennessee, Texas
Southern Reporter (So., So. 2d, So. 3d)	Alabama, Florida, Louisiana, Mississippi

Cases in the *South Western Reporter* are reprinted in *Kentucky Decisions. Kentucky Decisions* eliminates cases from other states found in the *South Western Reporter*, while retaining the same volume and page citation for each Kentucky case. The result is a set containing many fewer volumes, which is more practical for most attorneys practicing within the state.

III. Court Reporters

A. Parts of a Reported Case

A case printed in a reporter volume includes the language of the court's opinion as well as supplemental information supplied by the publisher of the reporter to aid the researcher in using the opinion. Figure 3-2 on the next page depicts a Kentucky case found in the *South Western Reporter*, illustrating the various parts of a published decision.

Case Name. The name of the case includes the names of the parties. In an appellate decision, the petitioner or the appellant is the first party named. This is the party who lost at the last proceeding and who is seeking the appeal. The appellee or the respondent is the party who won at the last proceeding and against whom the appeal is sought. The order of the parties in the case name does not indicate who was plaintiff or defendant in the original trial.

Docket Number. The docket number is a unique number assigned to a case when it is filed with the court. All documents filed in connection with the case within the same court are labeled with the same docket number.

Court. Since regional reporters contain opinions both of courts of last resort and also intermediate appellate courts for the states covered within the region, it is important to note from which court and jurisdiction the opinion was delivered.

Date. The case indicates the date on which the opinion was issued. For citation purposes, only the year the case was decided is important.

Synopsis. The synopsis is a short summary of the opinion written by the publisher's editors. Currently, the synopsis is divided into two parts: background and holding. (Older cases may only give the holding.) While the synopsis is useful for determining how relevant a case is, you should be careful to remember that it is not part of the opinion and should never be cited.

Headnotes. There may be several headnotes associated with an opinion. Each headnote is a short description of a point of law addressed by the court within its opinion. The headnotes associated with a case are numbered se-

Figure 3-2. Case Excerpt from *Carmical v. Bullock*, 251 S.W.3d 324 (Ky. App. 2008)

Court of Appeals of Kentucky.

John CARMICAL, Appellant
v.
Keith BULLOCK, Appellee.

← Parties and procedural designations

No. 2006-CA-001595-MR.

← Docket number

Aug. 10, 2007.
Discretionary Review Denied by
Supreme Court May 14, 2008.

Background: Home food delivery route manager sued customer for damages sustained as result of attack by customer's pet dog. Following jury trial in the Madison Circuit Court, Julia Hylton Adams, J., customer was found not liable for damages. Route manager appealed.

← Synopsis

Holding: The Court of Appeals, Wine, J., held that customer was not strictly liable for route manager's injuries.

Affirmed.

1. Negligence 303(1)
"Strict liability" is a judicial doctrine which relieves a plaintiff from proving specific acts of negligence and protects him from certain defenses.

← Headnote

2. Animals 65(4), 97
Even if statute pertaining to liability for property loss or injury by dog creates a strict liability action, negligence principles are still applicable, as a dog owner's liability should be subject to the doctrine of comparative negligence. KRS 258.275(1) (Repealed).

quentially and, at the place within the opinion where the point of law is discussed, the corresponding headnote number is inserted. As with the synopsis, headnote language is supplied by the publisher and should not be cited.

At the beginning of each headnote is a word or phrase, or several words or phrases, in bold print. These words and phrases provide subject access to the point of law in the headnote and are used in indexes, called *digests*, to locate other cases which address a similar point of law. In reporters published by West Publishing Company (now a division of Thomson Reuters), such as the *South Western Reporter*, the word or phrase is referred to as a *topic*. Topics are broad subject designations, which are subdivided into more specific subjects by *key numbers*.

Headnotes and the words and phrases that describe points of law are written by the publisher's editors. Therefore, these features will differ if the same case is consulted in a different publisher's reporter. The headnotes in West's *South Western Reporter* will be the same as those found on Westlaw and in other regional reporters. Headnotes used on Lexis will be different.

Attorneys. The names of the attorneys of record and the firms for which they worked appear just before the opinion.

Opinion. The name of the judge who wrote the opinion precedes the text of the opinion. The words "per curiam" may precede the text of the opinion if the opinion is to be credited to the court as a whole, rather than to an individual judge or justice. The majority opinion appears first. This is the opinion with which a majority of the judges agree. It determines the outcome of the case and has precedential value. Following the majority opinion may be one or more concurring opinions. These are written by judges who agree with the outcome of the majority opinion, but have reached that outcome from different reasoning. Following the majority opinion and any concurring opinions, there may appear dissenting opinions. Dissenting opinions are written by judges and justices who disagree with the majority.

B. Features of a Reporter Volume

At the front of West reporter volumes can be found a table listing the names of judges and justices assigned to courts within jurisdictions covered by the reporter volume. Also at the front of the volume are two *tables of cases*, or alphabetical listings of the cases found within the volume. One table of cases is a master list of all cases reported within the volume. The second is a table of cases listed by the jurisdictions covered by the reporter. For example, in the *South Western Reporter*, this second table of cases has separate lists of cases from Arkansas, Kentucky, Missouri, Tennessee, and Texas. The table of cases by jurisdiction within a volume of the *Federal Reporter* will list cases by federal circuit.

Table 3-3. Reporters for Federal Court Cases

Court	Reporter Name	Abbreviation
U.S. Supreme Court	*United States Reports* (official) *Supreme Court Reporter* *United States Supreme Court Reports, Lawyers' Edition*	U.S. S. Ct. L. Ed. or L. Ed. 2d
U.S. Courts of Appeals	*Federal Reporter*	F. or F.2d or F.3d
U.S. District Courts	*Federal Supplement*	F. Supp. or F. Supp. 2d or F. Supp. 3d

C. Advance Sheets

The bound volumes of reporters may take months to be published and distributed. To make cases available sooner, publishers issue *advance sheets*. These are softbound booklets containing the newest cases covered by the reporter. Advance sheets are temporary and, as each bound volume is received, it replaces several advance sheet booklets. The citation to a case in an advance sheet is the same as its citation will be once the bound volume is issued.

IV. Reporters for Federal Cases

So far, this chapter has dealt with reporters for Kentucky cases. This part explains the reporters for cases decided by federal courts. Table 3-3 lists the federal court reporters, along with their citation abbreviations.

A. United States Supreme Court Cases

Decisions of the United States Supreme Court are reported in *United States Reports*, which is the official reporter; *Supreme Court Reporter*, which is a West publication; and *United States Supreme Court Reports, Lawyers' Edition*, another unofficial reporter, published by LexisNexis. Although *United States Reports* is the official reporter, meaning that you should cite it if possible, that series frequently publishes cases several years after they are decided. Thus, recent cases will frequently be cited to the *Supreme Court Reporter*. Another source for finding recent cases from the Supreme Court is *United States Law Week*.

This service publishes the full text of cases from the Supreme Court and provides summaries of important decisions of state and federal courts.

There are a number of free online sources for Supreme Court opinions. The Court's website (https://www.supremecourt.gov/opinions/opinions.aspx) includes slip opinions within minutes after the decisions are rendered. Lexis, Westlaw, and Bloomberg Law provide quick access to Supreme Court opinions, as well as to briefs filed by the parties.

B. United States Court of Appeals Cases

Cases decided by the federal intermediate appellate courts are published in the *Federal Reporter*, now in its third series. Lexis, Westlaw, and Bloomberg Law include cases for federal courts of appeals in several databases. In addition, federal appeals courts maintain their own websites that provide access to cases.

C. United States District Court Cases

Since 1932, selected cases from the United States District Courts have been reported in the *Federal Supplement*. Opinions are also available on Lexis, Westlaw, and Bloomberg Law and also at the websites of each district.

V. Topical Reporters

Some reporters publish cases on a particular topic, rather than cases from a specific court or region. Examples of these include *Bankruptcy Reporter*, *West's Education Reporter*, and *United States Tax Cases*. Some of these may include opinions that are not available elsewhere. Often, these topical reporters include cases that are also included in various state and federal reporters. When this happens, it is important to consult your citation manual to be sure to cite to the proper source.

VI. Unreported Opinions

A great majority of court decisions are not reported at all. Very few state trial court decisions are reported. The result is that trials may become quite famous because of much news coverage, yet no opinion can be located. In addition, some appellate level state decisions may not be reported. The extent of reporting state opinions varies from state to state. Likewise, the majority of federal district court and intermediate court of appeals decisions are not reported.

Some unpublished opinions can be found on Lexis and Westlaw. They can also be located in a few print sources, such as the *Federal Appendix*. Many recent decisions can also be found on the website of the court issuing the opinion. Care must be taken in referring to unpublished opinions, as their precedential value may be limited. Some jurisdictions limit the impact of unpublished opinions, and others forbid citing to them altogether.

VII. Reading and Analyzing Cases[4]

After locating a case, you must read it, understand it, and analyze its potential relevance to the problem you are researching. This process may take more mental work than you have ever dedicated to just a few pages of text. It is not unusual for a lawyer to spend hours reading and re-reading a complex case. For a novice, this reading is frequently interrupted by referring to a law dictionary to try to understand the terms used.

To aid your early efforts at reading cases, the following sections explain basic concepts of civil procedure and case analysis. The chapter ends with strategies for reading cases effectively.

A. A Thimbleful of Civil Procedure

The person who believes he was harmed begins civil litigation by filing a complaint in the court he selects. The plaintiff is the person who files the complaint; the person against whom the complaint is filed is the defendant. The complaint names the parties, states the facts, notes the relevant laws, and asks for relief. Courts vary considerably in how much information is required at this stage of the litigation. In general, the complaint must be specific enough to put the defendant on notice of the legal concerns at issue and to allow her to prepare a defense.

The defendant has a limited amount of time in which to file a response to this complaint. (If the defendant does nothing within the prescribed time, the plaintiff can ask the court for a default judgment, which would grant the plaintiff the relief sought in the complaint.) One form of response to the complaint is an answer. In the answer, the defendant admits to the parts of the complaint that she knows are true, denies those things that she disputes, and asserts no knowledge of other allegations. The defendant may also raise affirmative defenses.

---

4. This part of the chapter is drawn from *Oregon Legal Research* by Suzanne E. Rowe and is used with permission.

Throughout the litigation, parties submit a variety of papers to the court for its consideration. Some require no action or response from the court, for example, the filing of the complaint. In other instances, a party asks the court to make a decision or take action. An example is a motion for summary judgment, where a party asks the court to decide in that party's favor without the need for a trial.

When the trial judge grants a motion that ends a case, the losing party can appeal. The appealing party is called the appellant; the other party is the respondent. In deciding an appeal from an order granting a motion, the appellate court is deciding whether the trial judge was correct in issuing the order at that stage of the litigation. If the appellate court agrees with the decision of the trial judge, it will affirm. If not, the court will reverse the order granting the motion and in some instances remand the case back to the trial court.

Even at trial, the parties might make motions that can be appealed. For example, during the trial, the plaintiff presents his evidence first. After all of the plaintiff's witnesses have testified, the defendant may move for a judgment as a matter of law, arguing that the plaintiff cannot win based on the evidence presented and asking for an immediate decision. An order granting that motion could be appealed.

Most reported cases are appeals of orders granting motions. These cases apply different standards of review, depending on the motion that is the object of the appeal. While standards of review are beyond the scope of this book, understanding the procedural posture of the case is crucial to understanding the court's holding. The relevant rules of civil procedure will guide your analysis. Texts listed in Appendix B of this book contain helpful explanations as well.

B. Analyzing the Substance of Cases

Early in your career it may be difficult to determine whether a case is relevant to your research problem. If the case concerns the same legally significant facts as your client's situation and the court applies law on point for your problem, then the case is relevant. Legally significant facts are those that affect the court's decision. Some attorneys call these outcome-determinative facts or key facts. Which facts are legally significant depends on the case. The height of the defendant in a contract dispute is unlikely to be legally significant, but that fact may be critical in a criminal case where the only eyewitness testified that the thief was about five feet tall.

Rarely will research reveal a case with facts that are exactly the same as your client's situation. Rather, several cases may involve facts that are similar to your client's situation but not exactly the same. Your job is to determine whether the facts are similar enough for a court to apply the law in the same way and reach the same outcome. If the court reached a decision favorable to your client, you will highlight the similarities. If, on the other hand, the court reached an unfavorable decision from your client's perspective, you may argue that the case is distinguishable from yours based on its facts or that its reasoning is faulty. You have an ethical duty to ensure that the court knows about a case directly on point, even if the outcome of that case is adverse to your client.

It is also unlikely that one case will address all aspects of your client's situation. Most legal claims have several elements or factors. Elements are required subparts of a claim, while factors are important aspects but not required. If a court decides that one element is not met, it may not discuss the others. In a different case, the court may decide that two factors are so overwhelming that others have no impact on the outcome. In these circumstances, you would have to find other cases that analyze the other elements or factors.

Once you determine that a case is relevant to some portion of your analysis, you must decide how heavily it will weigh in your analysis. Two important points need to be considered here. One is the concept of *stare decisis*; the other is the difference between the holding of the case and dicta within that case.

Stare decisis means "to stand by things decided." This means that courts must follow prior opinions, ensuring consistency in the application of the law. This requirement, however, is limited to the courts within one jurisdiction. The Court of Appeals of Kentucky must follow the decisions of the Kentucky Supreme Court, but not those of the courts of any other state. The concept of *stare decisis* also refers to a court with respect to its own opinions. The Court of Appeals, thus, should follow its own earlier cases in deciding new matters. A court (usually only the state's highest court) may decide not to continue following its earlier cases because of changes in society that have outdated that law or because a new statute has been enacted that changes the legal landscape.

Under *stare decisis*, courts are required to follow only the holding of prior cases. The holding is the court's ultimate decision on the matter of law at issue in the case. Other statements or observations included in the opinion are not binding; they are referred to as dicta. For example, a court in a property dispute may hold that the land belongs to Martinez. In reaching that decision, the court may note that had the facts been slightly different, it would have decided that the land belonged to Seifer. That observation is not binding on future courts, although it may be cited as persuasive authority.

After finding a number of cases that have similar facts, that discuss the same legal issue, and that are binding on your client, the next step is to synthesize the cases to state and explain the legal rule. Sometimes a court states the rule fully; if not, piece together the information from the relevant cases to state the rule completely but concisely. Then use the analysis and facts of various cases to explain the law. Decide how the rule applies to the client's facts, and determine your conclusion. Note that this method of synthesis is much more than mere summaries of all the various cases. Legal analysis texts in Appendix B of this book explain synthesis in detail.

C. Strategies for Reading Cases

The following strategies may help you in reading and analyzing case law.

Review the synopsis quickly to determine whether the case seems to be on point. If so, skim the headnotes to find the particular portion of the case that is relevant. Remember that one case may discuss several issues of law, only one or two of which may interest you. Go to the portion of the case identified by the relevant headnote and decide whether it is important for your project. If so, skim the entire case to get a feeling for what happened and why, focusing on the portion of the case identified by the relevant headnote.

Read the case slowly and carefully. Skip the parts that are obviously not pertinent to your problem. For example, when researching a property question, there is no need to scrutinize the tort issue that is not pertinent to your property question. At the end of each paragraph or page, consider what you have read. If you cannot summarize it, try reading the material again.

The next time you read the case, take notes. The notes may be in the form of a formal "case brief" or they may be scribbles that only you can understand. Regardless of the form, the process of taking notes will help you parse through, identify, and comprehend the essential concepts of the case. If you are a student, the notes will record your understanding of the case both for class discussion and for the end of the semester when you begin to review for exams. When preparing to write a legal document, the notes will assist you in organizing your analysis into an outline. Note that skimming text online or highlighting a printed page is often not sufficient to achieve thorough comprehension of judicial opinions.

Chapter 4

Finding Cases

With a citation, you can easily find a case online or in a set of reporters. However if you are trying to find a case by subject or by some other criterion, then you must consult another source to identify the case. This chapter discusses finding cases using digests as well as online methods of locating cases.

I. West Digests

A digest is a multi-volume set of books that acts as an index to court opinions. If you are looking for cases but do not have specific citations, you may consult a digest to find references to cases in reporters. This chapter's discussion concentrates on digests published by Thomson Reuters West division because they are the most widely used. Much of the information provided here would apply to any other case digests as well.

First, select the correct set of digests by jurisdiction and date. Kentucky cases decided from 1930 to the present are indexed in *Kentucky Digest 2d.* The first series of *Kentucky Digest* indexes cases decided before 1930. These digests include reported cases from state courts and federal cases originating in Kentucky that are reported in the *Federal Supplement*, the *Federal Reporter*, and the various reporters of cases decided by the United States Supreme Court.

West publishes other digests that correspond to almost all individual states; to some, although not all, regions; and to federal jurisdictions. There is a separate digest for United States Supreme Court cases. West's *Decennial Digest* indexes cases from all United States jurisdictions. The *Decennial Digest* may be helpful in print research when your library does not own a digest for a jurisdiction whose laws you are researching, or if you are looking for persuasive authority from other jurisdictions.

There are several parts to a set of digests, corresponding to various ways that a researcher may want to find cases. Volumes labeled Table of Cases provide citations to cases if the case name is known. Volumes labeled Words and Phrases cite cases in which a term or phrase is interpreted or defined by a court.

Most researchers use digests to find cases by subject. To begin a subject search in a digest, locate the volumes labeled Descriptive-Word Index. Look in the Descriptive-Word Index under keywords that describe the subject; these will be the research terms you generated in Chapter 1. Entries in the Descriptive-Word Index consist of an abbreviation for a topic and a key number. (See Chapter 3 for an explanation of topics and key numbers as a classification of points of law represented by headnotes in cases.)

In most of the digest volumes, the more than 450 topics are arranged alphabetically. The spine indicates which topics are included within each volume. Within each topic, key numbers representing topic subdivisions are arranged numerically. Using the reference from the Descriptive-Word Index, you will find headnotes to cases pertaining to the point of law being researched. An abbreviation identifies the court and date at the top of each headnote. At the bottom of each headnote is a citation to the case from which the headnote was taken.

Most digest volumes are updated by pocket parts, pamphlets stapled to a cardboard backing and slipped into a pocket in the back of the book. You should consult the pocket part of the relevant volumes of the Descriptive-Word Index to discover new topic and key number entries. Likewise, consult the pocket part for each topic volume to find headnotes to newer cases. *Decennial Digests* are updated by separate bound volumes called *General Digests*. Each volume of the *General Digest* is a separate digest unto itself. Every tenth volume of the *General Digest* contains a cumulative Descriptive-Word Index and Table of Cases for the previous ten volumes. In addition, each tenth volume contains a cumulative Table of Key Numbers that indicates in which of the previous ten volumes new headnotes can be found by topic and key number.

II. Online Topic Searching

Lexis, Westlaw, and Bloomberg Law allow searching for cases by subject using a variety of methods.

A. Topic and Key Number Searching Online

Because the *Kentucky Digest* is a West publication, only Westlaw will permit searching using the same topics and key numbers utilized by West reporters. On Westlaw, each West topic has been assigned a number. For example, the topic Adverse Possession has been assigned the number 20. To conduct a topic and key number search, you must convert the topic to its assigned number. If you know the key number and topic you wish to search, in the search box on any search screen for databases containing case law, type "adv:" then the topic number, the letter "k" and then the key number. For example, to find cases about boarding searches at airports, because the topic "searches and seizures" converts to the number 349 and searches occurring at airports are key number 72, one would type "**adv:349k72**."

If a researcher does not know which topic and key number applies, she or he should start at the home page and click on "browse." Under the All Content tab, a menu lists "Cases" and "Key Numbers" underneath "Cases." Click on Key Numbers and a menu of all topics is listed. Clicking on the topic name expands the menu to show all key numbers beneath the topic. Alternatively, an issue can be typed in the search box at the top of the topic menu (e.g., "airport boarding searches") and the system will provide suggested topics and key numbers.

B. Searching Using Terms and Connectors

One very effective method of finding cases on Westlaw, Lexis, and Bloomberg Law involves the use of terms and connectors. This process begins by identifying pertinent research terms as described in Chapter 1. Then you devise a search strategy by combining the terms using Boolean connectors, proximity connectors, fields, truncation, and wildcards to ensure that retrieved cases will be on point. See Chapter 11 for a detailed description of search strategies using terms and connectors.

By employing these devices in combination on legal research services, you can construct a specifically designed search strategy that is likely to retrieve cases that are relevant to your search subject. For example, assume you want to find newer court decisions that discuss parental immunity for liability to their children when they are injured as a result of an automobile accident. You might try a search similar to this: **(automo! or car or vehicle) w/10 (accident or crash or wreck) and parent! w/10 immun! and date(>2000)**.

In this example, the system will look for one of the synonyms for automobile within ten terms of one of the synonyms for accident. Truncating the root "automo" means that the words "automobile" and "automotive" will be retrieved. The parentheses around the synonyms group them and instruct the system to perform the "or" functions before applying the proximity connector. This is called *nesting*. So a case discussing a car accident and a case discussing an automobile wreck will be retrieved. In addition, somewhere in the case "parent" or "parental" must occur within ten terms of "immune" or "immunity." The date field search instructs the system that any case retrieved must be newer than the year 2000.

As a final step in the case law research process, you should always verify the authority of cases that you will rely upon, both to be sure that the opinion is the final disposition of the case and to be sure that later opinions have not adversely affected the legal issue for which you are using the case. (See Chapter 9.) Each online legal system has a service for this purpose: Shepard's Citations on Lexis, KeyCite on Westlaw, and BCite on Bloomberg Law.

C. Natural Language Searching

Lexis, Westlaw, and Bloomberg Law permit you to key in a plain English query to retrieve court decisions. While natural language searches may be more convenient for a researcher who is new to online searching, or who searches infrequently, the traditional terms and connectors search will often be more effective in retrieving a specific case. Terms and connectors sometimes allow the researcher to better define a search to hone in on a limited number of documents that better satisfy the query. See Chapter 11 for more information about natural language searching.

III. Kentucky Court Site

Aside from the commercial online legal systems, Kentucky court opinions can be found online by visiting the Kentucky Court of Justice website (http://apps.courts.ky.gov/supreme/sc_opinions.shtm). Published and unpublished opinions are available by entering search information in the menu to the left of the screen. The site includes detailed instructions regarding search protocols. Coverage includes Court of Appeals decisions from 1996 to the present and Supreme Court opinions from 1999 to the present. A combined search for opinions of both courts may be performed. In addition to opinions, other court information such as dockets, forms, rules of practice, and records can be found at http://courts.ky.gov.

IV. Casemaker

Lawyers licensed in Kentucky have access to Casemaker through the Kentucky Bar Association website (http://www.kybar.org/). After logging in with their bar numbers, these lawyers can access cases dating back to 1948 from Kentucky and several other states. Casemaker search protocols are more rudimentary than those used by the commercial services, and decisions on Casemaker lack editorial features such as headnotes.

Chapter 5

Statutes

Statutes are written laws created by legislative bodies. Although the foundation of the American legal system is the common law, its current structure has been substantially enlarged by statutes. Significant areas of law like crime and punishment, health care, taxation, consumer protection, domestic relations, and the environment are regulated by statutes. New statutes have been written to address new societal concerns or technological advances. Moreover, significant areas of the common law have been codified (made into statutes) to make the law more transparent and understandable to the public or to make it more rational and easily applied to modern circumstances. In areas still largely governed by the common law, like tort law, statutes nonetheless govern major procedural issues, including matters like jurisdiction, service of process, and statutes of limitation. Because of this, every research project must include a survey of applicable statutes.

This chapter provides general information about statutory research in Kentucky, explains how to research statutes in print and online, explores statutory interpretation, and touches on researching statutes in other jurisdictions. It is important to note that the term "statute" is used somewhat imprecisely at times. The term can sometimes refer to a large piece of legislation with many sections like the "trademark statute." However, when lawyers use the term, they are typically referring to a smaller, distinct section of law like 17 U.S.C. § 107, which outlines the copyright fair use provision. It is in this second sense that this chapter uses the term.

I. Kentucky Statutory Research

Kentucky statutes are enacted by the Kentucky General Assembly, a bicameral legislative body that includes a House of Representatives and a smaller Senate. The Kentucky legislature meets for 60 days at the beginning of even-numbered years and 30 days in odd-numbered years. Laws typically become effective 90 days after the end of the session, usually sometime in the summer.[1] The first place laws are available is on the legislature's website (http://www.lrc.ky.gov); later the laws of the session are published in volumes of the annual *Kentucky Acts*. Eventually they are folded into the Kentucky Revised Statutes, the official state code of laws. For more detail on this process, see Chapter 6, Legislative History.

A. Kentucky Revised Statutes

The Kentucky Revised Statutes (KRS) is the official code of all permanent laws of a general nature in force in Kentucky. The official version of the KRS is an internal electronic database maintained by the legislature's administrative arm, the Legislative Research Commission (LRC). Until 1969, the legislature published a printed edition of the KRS but discontinued that practice, deciding to certify one or more of the available commercially published versions.

The LRC is empowered to certify a version of the KRS as official if it meets certain legal requirements. To obtain certification, Kentucky law requires that the publication contain "the text of all laws contained in the official version" of the KRS, as well as copies of the Kentucky and U.S. constitutions, the rules of the Supreme Court of Kentucky, the Kentucky Rules of Civil Procedure, and the Kentucky Rules of Criminal Procedure, and "[a]ny annotations, historical notes, and other information" that the compiler "deems appropriate to include."[2] Certified editions must contain a "full and accurate index" of the statute laws and state constitution, and must "be updated in a manner and frequency acceptable to the Commission."[3] If the LRC has determined that a particular edition meets these criteria, that edition will contain a certificate issued by the director of the LRC in the front of volume one.[4]

The KRS is made up of 44 titles, which are divided into chapters, and further into sections. However, for the purpose of citation, only chapters and sections are relevant. Citations are made up of the chapter, a decimal point, and a three-digit number representing the relevant section of that chapter. See Table 5-1 for the example of the sections under one chapter.

---

1. Ky. Const. § 55. Bills designated as emergency legislation and passed by an absolute majority of both houses become law upon the signature of the governor.

2. KRS 7.134. This is the common format in Kentucky for citations to the KRS. See Appendix A of this book for a more detailed explanation of state citation rules.

3. *Id.*

4. *Id.*

Table 5-1. Sections in Chapter 513: Arson

Chapter 513 Arson and Related Offenses
513.010 Definition of "building."
513.020 Arson in the first degree.
513.030 Arson in the second degree.
513.040 Arson in the third degree.
513.060 Burning personal property to defraud insurer.

B. Annotated Codes

Two separate annotated codes are designated as official versions of the KRS, *Michie's Kentucky Revised Statutes*, published by LexisNexis, and *Baldwin's Kentucky Revised Statutes*, published by Thomson Reuters' West division. Both versions are also annotated codes; this means that each section is annotated with references to related laws, judicial decisions, and secondary sources.

The two annotated codes have common features. Each code enhances each discrete statutory section with case annotations. These are lists of cases that cite the code section; each annotation consists of a citation to a case and a short summary of the case and how the court interpreted the statute in light of the facts of the case. Case annotations lead to cases, which are the primary tool lawyers use for interpreting the language of statutes. See Table 5-2 for an example of a case annotation to a statute.

The annotated codes also have summaries of the published opinions of the attorney general, who is often asked to interpret statutes for state agencies, local governments, and members of the legislature. In addition, both codes collect references to the statute in secondary materials, particularly Kentucky publications like the Kentucky Bar Association journal *Bench & Bar*, Kentucky

Table 5-2. Sample Annotation, KRS 511.020, First-Degree Burglary

The first degree burglary statute, KRS 511.020, applies to every structure that fits the definition of a building as used in common parlance, and the 1980 amendments to this statute broaden its scope to encompass "buildings" and not just "dwellings," so that an uninhabited, condemned, and abandoned building in which a murder victim's body was found is included under the burglary statute. *Funk v. Com.* (Ky. 1992) 842 S.W.2d 476.

Printed with permission of West, a Thomson Reuters business.

law reviews, and legal treatises like the *Kentucky Practice* series. Savvy researchers know that the publishers of each code are more likely to cite to treatises in their product line and will, when possible, check annotations to both codes. Each code section is annotated with a variety of notes on the legislative history of the statute (see Chapter 6), and, depending on the context, with cross-references to other sections of the KRS.

Both codes are also updated with annual pocket parts and semi-annual supplements, one of which is a version of the session laws of the latest meeting of the state legislature, the *Kentucky Acts*. However, because the publishers are dependent upon the legislature to certify all changes, the pocket parts are often published months after the effective dates of the laws passed in the latest session of the legislature. See the section "Updating Statutes" later in this chapter.

1. Michie's Kentucky Revised Statutes

Michie's Kentucky Revised Statutes was started by the Bobbs-Merrill Company in 1971 but soon was acquired by Michie Company. It is currently published by LexisNexis and is certified by the LRC as an official edition.

Michie's KRS is published in a hardbound book format with pocket parts. There are currently 36 hardbound volumes in the set, with a three-volume softbound rules service, and a two-volume softbound index. The set is updated with annual pocket parts and a semi-annual advance service. In addition, an Advance Legislative Service is published after each session of the Kentucky General Assembly containing the session laws of that body. There is a five-page "User's Guide" in the first volume.

2. Baldwin's Kentucky Revised Statutes Annotated

The pedigree of *Baldwin's Kentucky Revised Statutes Annotated* dates back to 1915 when the Baldwin Law Book Co. purchased John D. Carroll's *Kentucky Statutes*, then the semi-official statutory code of Kentucky. The set later took on the name of editor-publisher William Edward Baldwin. In 1979, Baldwin's KRS was certified as an official edition by the LRC. The Baldwin's name was retained as a brand-name when West Publishing Company bought the Banks-Baldwin Company in 1993, a practice continued by current owner Thomson Reuters.

Baldwin's KRS is published in 41 hardbound volumes, with softbound index volumes. It is updated with annual pocket parts and semi-annual advance sheets. Baldwin's issues separate softbound *Acts* volumes after every regular or special session of the Kentucky General Assembly. A detailed fifteen-page "User's Guide" is included in the first volume of the set.

C. Researching the Kentucky Revised Statutes in Print

The best method for researching Kentucky statutes depends on what information you have before beginning. If you know what statute or range of statutes is involved, perhaps from court papers or case law research, then you can go directly to the KRS and find that statute by looking at the information printed on the spine of each volume. When researching statutes this way, you should take care to examine the statutes before and after the one you are checking. There may be definitional statutes, procedural provisions, and other parts of the statutory scheme that are vital to a full understanding of your primary statute's operation. To be thorough, flip backward to find the directory of statutes for the chapter in which your statute is found. Refer back to Table 5-1 for an example.

When you start to research without knowing a specific statute, a different method is necessary. Here you will need to check to see if your client's factual situation and the legal issues are covered by Kentucky's statutes. In this case, the following steps may be useful.

1. Create a List of Research Terms

It always helps to plan your statutory research by developing a possible list of keywords that is as complete as possible to check against indexes and finding aids. Be sure to include all synonyms and be aware that Kentucky may use different terminology for legal issues than other states. A legal dictionary or thesaurus may be helpful.

2. Search the Index

The next step is to take your list of terms to the index volumes of one of Kentucky's official statutory codes. Both currently have two softbound index volumes at the end of the set. In addition, there is a separate index at the end of each volume in the set and special indexes for the Kentucky constitution and rules of court.

Make a thorough search of the index because more than one heading in the index may relate to your topic and several statutes may apply. Be sure to follow cross-references. Write down all the other statutes that may relate to your statute. See Table 5-3 for an example of a portion of an index section.

Table 5-3. Selected Entries for Arson in the Michie's KRS Index

Buildings, defined, § 513.010
Defenses, use of deadly force to defend property, § 503.080
Definitions, § 513.010
First degree, Class A felony, § 513.020
First degree, elements, § 513.020
Insurance, burning personal property to defraud insurer, § 513.060
Second degree, Class B felony, § 513.030
Second degree, elements, § 513.030
Third degree, Class D felony, § 513.040
Third degree, elements, § 513.040

Reprinted with the permission of LexisNexis.

3. Find and Read Statutory Language

Both the Michie's and Baldwin's KRS sets contain the text of each statute, arranged in numeric order and with clear location information printed on the spines of each volume of the set.

Find the statutes based on the numbers you took down earlier in your research and read the statutes carefully. Think about their meaning and how they may apply to the facts of your client's case. You may have to read them a couple of times to determine their full meaning. Be sure to read other statutes in the same chapter.

To fully understand a statute it is sometimes useful to break it down into its component parts in outline or bullet-point format. Words like "and" and "or" are key to determining the meaning of statutes and are typically used to include or exclude persons or situations for the scope of a statute. Note also that the words "may" and "shall" convey precise legal meanings not as clear in everyday language. When a statute uses the word "may" it means the action is permitted. When it uses the word "shall" the action is required. See Table 5-4, for an example of how a statute can be reduced to its elements.[5]

---

5. The exact language of KRS 513.020(1) is printed below.

(1) A person is guilty of arson in the first degree when, with intent to destroy or damage a building, he starts a fire or causes an explosion, and;

(a) The building is inhabited or occupied or the person has reason to believe the building may be inhabited or occupied; or

(b) Any other person sustains serious physical injury as a result of the fire or explosion or the firefighting as a result thereof.

Table 5-4. Outline of KRS 513.020(1), Arson in the First Degree

(1) A person is guilty of arson in the first degree when
- with the intent to
    - destroy OR damage
    - a building, he
- starts a fire OR causes an explosion AND
- (a) the building is
    - inhabited OR
    - occupied OR
    - he has reason to believe it is occupied or inhabited; OR
- (b) any other person sustains serious physical injury
    - as a result of the fire OR explosion OR
    - firefighting as a result thereof.

If your prior results found any definitional statutes, apply them to your analysis. There is also a general definitions section that applies to all Kentucky statutes at KRS 446.010. See a brief selection of general definitions in Table 5-5.

4. Updating Statutes

For many states, updating a print statutory code merely involves checking pocket parts and the advance supplements. However, thorough research in Kentucky involves taking a few more steps because—to put it bluntly—delays in the state legislature's codification process mean that new laws often go into effect before certified versions have been printed or uploaded to online services.

Table 5-5. Excerpts from KRS 446.010, Definitions for Statutes Generally

As used in the statute laws of this state, unless the context requires otherwise

(1) "Action" includes all proceedings in any court of this state;

(2) "Animal" includes every warm-blooded living creature except a human being;

(3) "Attorney" means attorney-at-law;

(4) "Bequeath" and "devise" mean the same thing;

(5) "Bequest" and "legacy" mean the same thing, and embrace either real or personal estate, or both;

(6) "Cattle" includes horse, mule, ass, cow, ox, sheep, hog, or goat of any age or sex.

As noted earlier, Kentucky's legislature meets annually in either a 30-day or 60-day session at the beginning of the year, roughly between January and April. Laws usually become effective around June or July. They are available online, but it is not until the legislature's codification office finishes its work that the official revision of the code is provided to the publishers of the two official codes. In August or September, the official "session laws" of the legislature, the *Kentucky Acts*, is published. (The session laws are the final versions of each piece of legislation enacted in that session of the legislature). The official state compiler then certifies the changed sections of the KRS and only then sends them to Thomson Reuters (which uploads them onto Westlaw and begins to edit them into the pocket parts of Baldwin's KRS) and to LexisNexis (which does the same for its online service and print Michie's KRS). Finally, in October or November the annual pocket parts are issued, frequently containing laws that have been effective for two or three months.

To make sure that you are applying the most up-to-date law, you will need to follow a number of steps. Initially, check the statute's citation in the pocket part of the volume you are using. (Pocket parts are pamphlets found in a pocket in the back of the book. Generally only the parts of a law that are changed are found in the pocket part, but new laws are published in full). If there has been no intervening session of the legislature you are finished; however, if you are researching any time after May, it is best to check a few more sources.

First, check to see if there is a legislative supplement with the *Kentucky Acts* of the legislature that is dated sometime after the copyright date of the pocket parts. This supplement should be easy to find as it is much larger than the other supplements. In the back, a table lists KRS sections that have been changed. If there is no *Acts* supplement, but you are researching in late summer or early fall, there is one more step a prudent researcher should take. Go to the Kentucky legislature's website (http://www.lrc.ky.gov). Choose "Kentucky Law" from the left navigation panel. From here choose "KY Acts." From the main "Acts" page, click the "Acts Tables" link for the latest session. Then, choose the "Table of KRS Sections Affected" link and look up your KRS section in the table. Check the "Acts Disposition Table" link to find the projected KRS citation.

5. Finding Related Cases

Finding a relevant statute is not the end of the research process. The next step is to find out if there is case law that interprets that statute, particularly precedents that apply that statute to fact patterns and legal situations similar to those of your client. Interpreting a statute is a daunting process, and judges are interested in any guidance from other courts.

The two official annotated codes are the obvious place to begin this stage of research. Each has collected cases that reference a particular statute and in most instances have arranged these cases by topic. Take care to look for cases interpreting not only the specific statute, but also related statutes before and after it in the code. Pocket parts collect new cases and should always be checked.

One other useful tool for finding case law on Kentucky statutes is the Statute Edition of *Shepard's Kentucky Citations*. This work has case citations to not only current KRS sections, but also the state constitution and rules of court. Older, pre-1942 codes are covered as well as the *Kentucky Acts*. *Shepard's Kentucky Citations* is updated quarterly. However, remember that citations only reflect judge-made law: this resource will not alert you to changes in a statute that have been made by the legislature.

6. Other Features of Annotated Codes

In order to be certified, a Kentucky statutory code must also contain the Constitution of the United States, the Constitution of Kentucky, the rules of the Supreme Court of Kentucky, the Kentucky Rules of Civil Procedure, and the Kentucky Rules of Criminal Procedure. Although it is not required under the certification statute, both KRS publishers liberally annotate these sections with case notes and citations to secondary materials. Both codes also include copies of historical documents like the Declaration of Independence, the Cession from Virginia, and Kentucky's three previous constitutions.

D. Kentucky Statutes Online

1. Kentucky Revised Statutes on the Internet

The LRC maintains an unofficial version of the KRS on its website (http://www.lrc.ky.gov/statutes/). This web-based KRS cautions that it does "not constitute an official text of the statutes" and that it is "intended for informational purposes only." The LRC says that it attempts to update this version as soon as is feasible after each session of the legislature.

The web version of the KRS can be accessed by drilling down from the title and chapters tables starting at the main page. You can also search for keywords and phrases from the main LRC search engine, limiting the search to the KRS with a drop-down menu. Search results are to PDF documents, each with the text of a single KRS section. While this means that a complex search returns dozens of hits, the compact nature of the web KRS makes it a handy resource to consult with an iPad or web-enabled mobile phone.

2. Kentucky Statutes on Casemaker

Casemaker is a legal database available to all lawyers licensed in Kentucky as a part of their dues. It is sponsored by the Kentucky Bar Association and is accessible through their website (http://www.kybar.org). To use Casemaker, a lawyer must first establish an account by logging into the website with her bar association ID number. The Casemaker website is fairly rudimentary compared with Lexis and Westlaw. The Kentucky statutes database is unannotated but is somewhat easier to search than the free LRC-sponsored KRS. Statutes can be searched satisfactorily in Casemaker's Kentucky cases database by putting the full citation of the statute in quotes.

II. Applying and Interpreting Kentucky Statutes

The Kentucky legislature gives general instructions as to how statutes are to be interpreted. KRS 446.080(1) directs that "statutes of this state shall be liberally construed with a view to promote their objects and carry out the intent of the legislature" noting also the traditional rule that "statutes in derogation of the common law are to be strictly construed *shall not* apply to the statutes of this state."

The legislature also dictates that the language of its statutes "be construed according to the common and approved usage of language," while at the same time accepting that "technical words and phrases, and such others as may have acquired a peculiar and appropriate meaning in the law" should be construed as such.[6] In order to assist in construction of the language of statutes, KRS 446.010 defines a number of terms commonly used in legislation. In addition, many specific definition statutes are placed throughout the KRS.

Kentucky's constitution, section 19(1), requires that no "ex post facto law" shall be enacted. Because of this, Kentucky statutes are not to be construed to have a retroactive effect, "unless expressly so declared."[7] However, to prevent persons charged with a crime from claiming that the offense they are charged with is no longer a crime, KRS 446.110 states that "[n]o new law shall be construed to repeal a former law as to any offense," unless the legislature clearly states that it intends that retroactive effect.[8]

6. KRS 446.080(4).
7. KRS 446.080(3).
8. KRS 446.110.

The statutes provide a number of rules to assist courts in rectifying errors in legislation. If two acts are enacted in the same session, the last one passed shall prevail.[9] However, if a law is repealed and amended in the same session, the law is deemed to have been repealed.[10] Recognizing that printing errors are inevitable, the legislature has passed rules to remedy the failure to underline new language,[11] the failure to indicate deleted material,[12] and to correct errors in a bill presented to the governor.[13] Other such provisions deal with effect of delayed repeal,[14] delayed amendment,[15] and delayed effective dates.[16]

When one section of a large piece of legislation is ruled unconstitutional by a court, the next question that arises is whether the whole law is invalid or whether only the unconstitutional part can be "severed" from the law. KRS 446.090 addresses this issue, by stating that it is "the intent of the General Assembly, in enacting any statute, that if any part of the statute be held unconstitutional the remaining parts shall remain in force, unless the statute provides otherwise," or if the remaining parts are "so essentially and inseparably connected" with the unconstitutional part to be "incapable of being executed" without that part.

Researchers seeking a good resource to assist in interpreting statutes should consult the *Bill Drafting Manual of the Kentucky General Assembly* (Legislative Research Commission 2011) or *Sutherland Statutes and Statutory Construction* (7th ed., Thomson Reuters 2010), the standard treatise on the topic.

III. Writing about Statutes

After analyzing your statute, you will often have to convey that analysis in writing. In doing so, you will wish to carefully and plainly show the application of the statutes you find to the facts of your client's case.

In order to ensure that your analysis is readable, clear, and concise, avoid block quotes to the statute. Quote only those parts of the statute that are most relevant to your analysis. Those parts that do not apply to the facts of your

9. KRS 446.250.
10. KRS 446.260.
11. KRS 446.270.
12. KRS 446.280.
13. KRS 446.310.
14. KRS 446.290.
15. KRS 446.300.
16. KRS 446.320.

case should be omitted. You should paraphrase the statute whenever possible, quoting only short phrases that are vital to the interpretation of the statute. This is especially true if quoting requires you to use many ellipses to indicate omissions.

It is important to begin your analysis with a short statement of the issue your client's case presents. Then you should briefly describe the statutes uncovered by your research and apply them to the facts of the case. Finally, you should conclude your analysis with language unambiguously resolving the question.

IV. Researching the Statutes of Other States

The basic process of researching Kentucky statute law can be applied, with some regional variation, to the statutory law of other states. Commercially published annotated codes are available for all 50 states, although some states also have unannotated official codes. All state codes are available on Lexis, Westlaw, and Bloomberg Law.

All U.S. states have unofficial online versions of their statutory materials. These can be easily found by searching Google for the state's name and the keywords "code" or "statutes." The Casemaker database also has statutes for all the states and session laws for all the states that participate in the consortium of state bar associations that manage it.

V. Federal Statutes

Federal statutes cover many matters that are litigated by Kentucky lawyers, both in the federal courts situated in Kentucky and in Kentucky courts under the principal of concurrent jurisdiction. For example, a party claiming racial discrimination can file a lawsuit in state court claiming that the defendant violated their rights under the Kentucky and federal civil rights acts. The court would then apply federal precedents to the federal claim and state law to the state claim.

The government-published *United States Code* is the official text of the federal statutes, but its slow publication schedule and its lack of case annotations make it rarely used by legal researchers. It is available in print and online on Congress.gov (http://uscode.house.gov). Far more used are the Thomson Reuters produced *United States Code Annotated* (USCA), also available on Westlaw, and the LexisNexis published *United States Code Service* (USCS), also available on Lexis.

The federal statutes are codified under 54 titles. Within each title, individual statutes are assigned section numbers. To cite a federal statute, include both the title and section number. The federal statute defining fair use under federal copyright law is 17 U.S.C. § 107 (2012); title 17 is devoted to copyright law, and 107 is the section number assigned to this statute. The date of publication of that volume of U.S.C. was 2012.

Both of the commercial codes contain the text of federal statutes annotations that refer the researcher to cases interpreting or applying each federal statute. Some researchers feel that USCA provides more case annotations than USCS, while USCS provides more helpful tables and better information on court rules. Often the two are of equal value so use whichever one is available. In addition to case annotations, they both have notes on the legislative history of the statute, cross-references to related code sections, and references to secondary sources discussing the statute.

The annotated codes are updated through pocket parts and paperback supplements. The federal annotated codes also contain annotated versions of the U.S. Constitution and of the federal rules of court.

Chapter 6

Legislative History

Often the surest guide to the interpretation of a statute is the documents created during the process of the law's enactment. The collection and analysis of these documents is commonly referred to as legislative history. Knowledge of legislative history is important for lawyers who seek to determine the meaning of ambiguous provisions of a statute and find interpretations favorable to their clients. Many Kentucky attorneys believe that when a case turns on the interpretation of a statute, due diligence requires that the statute's legislative history be thoroughly researched, even when they suspect nothing useful will be found.

This chapter begins with a brief description of how a bill becomes a law in Kentucky. Next, techniques for researching the legislative history of an enacted law are discussed. Finally, the chapter briefly describes how to track the progress of a bill in a current legislative session.

I. The Legislative Process

The Kentucky General Assembly is made up of the House of Representatives, consisting of 100 members elected to two-year terms, and the Senate, consisting of 38 members, elected to six-year terms.

The General Assembly is a "citizen's legislature" and meets for only 60 days (from January to April) in even-numbered years, and for only 30 days (from January to March) in odd-numbered years. The governor has the power to convene extraordinary sessions (commonly known as "special" sessions) to act on a topic or topics clearly outlined in the written proclamation calling the session. The leadership of the House and Senate meet each summer in non-legislative meetings known as "interim" conferences, but none of the legislature's constitutional powers can be exercised between sessions.

The state legislature has an administrative arm, the Legislative Research Commission (LRC), which researches problems that may be the subject of legislation, assists in the drafting of bills, codifies statutes, and oversees the General

Assembly's website (http://www.lrc.ky.gov). The LRC also publishes the official session laws, the journals of the House and Senate, and a number of informational publications. Among its regular titles are a number of documents helpful for understanding the Kentucky legislative process, including the *Bill Drafting Manual* and the web-based tutorial, "How a Bill Becomes Law" (http://www.lrc.ky.gov/legproc/how_law.htm). The LRC also publishes an annual publication, the *Kentucky General Assembly Directory*, which describes the leadership and committee structure for the session and has entries on all state legislators, including a photo and a brief biography.

The process for enacting a law bears some similarity to that of the U.S. Congress and other states, but Kentucky lawmaking is more heavily circumscribed by the state constitution than is true in other jurisdictions. For example, the provisions of a Kentucky statute must all be on the same general subject and that subject must be described by the statute's title. This means that the multi-subject "omnibus legislation" frequently passed by the U.S. Congress would be unconstitutional in Kentucky.

Table 6-1 shows the basic path of a bill from its introduction until it becomes an enacted statute, noting documents created along the way.

II. Kentucky Legislative History Research

Given the complexity of the legislative process and the political compromises inherent in lawmaking, it is not surprising that the enacted statute is occasionally subject to differing interpretations. Legislative history helps lawyers and judges understand the law by looking at the documents created when it was passed. It is not possible, however, to do the sort of detailed legislative history for a Kentucky statute that one traditionally does for a federal law because the Kentucky legislature does not publish transcripts of legislative debates or the reports of committees—the basic materials of federal legislative history. However, there are some official and unofficial sources that a researcher can use to at least understand the context of a statute and possibly shed some light on why the law was passed.

A. Sources of Kentucky Legislative History

As Kentucky does not publish committee reports or floor debates, the primary documents for legislative history research are texts that record the various versions of the bill as it passed through the legislative process. These works include the *Kentucky Acts*, which publishes the final enacted version of the law;

Table 6-1. How a Bill Becomes a Law

Legislative Action	Documents Produced
A legislator, a citizen, or a group suggests an idea for a law. A legislator agrees to sponsor a bill embodying the idea and asks the LRC staff to draft the language of the law. The bill can be pre-filed (if it is drafted in between sessions) or filed at any time in the session.	The bill is uploaded to the LRC website.
The bill is introduced in the House or the Senate. It receives the first of three readings and is assigned to a committee.	During the session, all actions, including readings and committee assignments, are reported in the daily *Legislative Record*; after the session, the *House Journal* and *Senate Journal* record them for posterity.
The committee can hold hearings on the bill, amend it, or hold a vote to either pass or not pass the bill. Committee chairs are very powerful in Kentucky and can kill a bill without hearings or a vote.	The minutes of committees are available for inspection in Frankfort.
If the bill is approved by the committee, it goes back to the full chamber for its second and third readings. The chamber can amend the bill, send it back to committee, or vote to pass or kill the bill.	Amendments to bills are loaded on the LRC website. Records of roll call votes can be found in the *House Journal* and *Senate Journal*.
If the bill is passed, it is sent to the other chamber, where the process is repeated.	
If there are differences between the versions of the bill passed in each chamber, a conference committee is appointed by the leadership to resolve differences in a substitute bill. The conference's substitute bill must be approved by a vote of both chambers.	The conference substitute is loaded on the LRC website.
The final bill is signed by the leaders of both chambers and sent to the governor.	The version of the bill sent to the governor is known as the enrolled bill.
The governor has ten days to veto the bill, sign it, or let the bill become law without his signature. If the bill is vetoed, the legislature can override the veto with a simple majority in both chambers.	The final bill is entered into the executive journal of the state maintained by the secretary of state.
All the enacted laws of the session are assigned chapter numbers in order of when they were passed.	The LRC collects these session laws and publishes them as the *Kentucky Acts*.
The staff of the LRC "codifies" the laws by assigning them a number that places them with other laws on similar subjects. The director of the LRC then "certifies" the codified laws as official and releases them to the two companies that publish editions of the Kentucky Revised Statutes.	Kentucky statutes are codified as the Kentucky Revised Statutes. Both LexisNexis' *Michie's Kentucky Revised Statutes* and Thomson Reuters' *Baldwin's Kentucky Revised Statutes* are official codes of Kentucky law.

the legislature's website, which offers access to bills and amendments; and the *House Journal* and *Senate Journal*, which record the daily activities of both chambers of the legislature.

1. Kentucky Acts

The LRC publishes all enacted statutes of a session of the General Assembly in a hardbound set of books called the *Kentucky Acts.* All bills and joint or concurrent resolutions[1] enacted during the session are collected and assigned chapter numbers based on the order that they were filed with the secretary of state. The volumes are indexed and a disposition table is included to indicate where the acts are placed in the Kentucky Revised Statutes (KRS).

2. Kentucky Journals

The *House Journal* and *Senate Journal* are prepared after the legislative session is over and record the daily activity of each body during the session, including the text of amendments and roll call votes. However, debate on the floor of the legislature is not recorded. Each journal has detailed tables and indexes that are vital to following the legislative history of a statute.

A related title is the *Legislative Record.* A tabloid newspaper that is published only when the General Assembly is in session, the *Record* records the daily status of bills and resolutions. The last issue shows the final executive action on each bill and is an important tool in the months between the end of the session and the publication of the hardbound journals.

3. Kentucky Legislative Research Commission Website

The main attraction of the LRC website is the full-text versions of bills and resolutions pending in the Kentucky General Assembly, but the site also contains a wealth of information about the legislative process. The current legislative calendar and schedule of monthly committee meetings are prominently posted, along with the rules of the House and Senate. Committee assignments and contact information on members are listed, along with data on LRC and other legislative staff persons. The online *Legislative Record*, a daily log of the flow of legislation, is also available. An online database based on the *Legislative*

---

1. A resolution expresses the opinion of the legislature. While resolutions of only one chamber have no force of law, joint resolutions are passed by both chambers and are legally binding. Concurrent resolutions, which are passed by one chamber and assented to by the other, are also binding in certain circumstances.

Record Final Action issues since 1986 and the latest *Legislative Record* can be searched by keyword to determine the final disposition of legislation.

a. Bills and Resolutions

During the period leading up to a regular or extraordinary session of the General Assembly, pre-filed bills and resolutions are placed on the LRC site. These are later supplemented by bills filed within the session. After the session adjourns, the final version of all bills filed remains on the website, listed by the date of the session.

b. Legislative Documents

Several documents on the legislative process are available through the LRC, including short pieces on legislative history, legislative terminology, and Kentucky's budget process. Summaries of Interim Studies and Reports are provided, along with links to relevant pre-filed legislation. Lists of the titles of the LRC's Informational Bulletin and Research Reports series are provided, along with the full text of some of the more popular titles.

B. Researching Legislative History Online and in Print

The basic process for researching a Kentucky law begins with a close reading of history notes in the KRS, continues with an examination of the session law in the *Kentucky Acts*, and then ends with a careful analysis of the course the law took from the time it was filed to the time it was enacted, using either the official journals of the House and Senate, or, in the case of laws passed after 1998, the electronic record on the website of the legislature.

During your research process, take careful notes of the dates of a law's enactment, its three readings, any votes, and the law's final passage. You should copy the language of the bill as introduced and any amendments along the way. The removal or addition of language to a statute can often aid in statutory interpretation. For example, when the legislature affirmatively removes a provision from a bill before passage, no later court is going to interpret that provision back into the final law. Conversely, a court will likely presume that language added to legislation just before passage was likely to be integral to its enactment and should not be severed by judicial ruling.

In order to research the enactment history of a particular section of a Kentucky statute, first jot down the enactment date and citation to the *Kentucky Acts* found in parentheses after the text in the KRS. For example, "2001, ch. 384, § 141, effective June 17, 2001" indicates the session law is found in Chapter 384, Section 141 of the 2001 edition of *Kentucky Acts*.

Table 6-2. Sample Entry from History of House Bills

Bill No.	Introduced	Referred	1st Read.	2nd Read.	3rd Read.	Sub.or Amend	Voting …	… Senate Mess.	Concur activities	Enrolled (to Gov.)	Other Action
HB45	9	14	75	79	165	79, 166	337	1243		1288, 1356	48, 56, 188

Go to the relevant volume of the *Kentucky Acts* to see how the section appeared in the original legislation. Sometimes the compilers of the KRS omit extraneous material useful to interpretation of a statute. In addition, an analysis of the organization of the original law may place the section you are researching into a context not apparent from its place in the revised code. In some cases, the act may have a preamble that explains its legislative purpose.

At the head of the act is the bill number, usually HB (House Bill) or SB (Senate Bill) followed by a number. An HB title means the law originated in the House, while an SB title means the law started in the Senate. This number is the key to researching the statute's history.

At this point, your options depend on when the law was passed. If the law was passed after 1998, you may be able do all your research on the Kentucky legislature's website (http://www.lrc.ky.gov). If the law was passed before 1998, you will need to visit a library that has access to good sets of the *Kentucky Acts* and *House Journal* and *Senate Journal*.

1. Researching Laws Passed Before 1998 in Print

If the law was passed before 1998, take the bill number to the appropriate year of the *House Journal* or *Senate Journal* (depending on which body originated the law). After finding the relevant journal, examine the appendices at the end of the last volume in the set for a table entitled "History of House Bills" (or "History of Senate Bills"). For example, if your law was passed in 1995 and is numbered "HB45," you would go to the 1995 *House Journal* and look for HB45 in the "History of House Bills" table.

The table notes the pages in the journal where important steps in the legislative process are discussed. Thus, in the sample entry in Table 6-2, HB 45 was introduced on page 9, referred to committee on page 14, had its first reading on page 75, was amended on pages 79 and 166, the vote was recorded on page 337, was sent to the Senate on page 1243, and was sent to the governor on page 1356.

Once you have fully researched the bill in the originating body, take your bill number to the journal of the other chamber and use the history tables there to do the same research in that journal. Be sure to copy the original bill and any amendments to the text.

2. Researching Laws Passed After 1998 Online

To research laws passed after 1998, go to the LRC website. Click "Legislation" on the top navigation bar. This will bring up a webpage with links to current and past sessions of the General Assembly. Click "Past Legislative Records" to bring up a list of regular and special sessions back to the May 1998 special session. Click the link for the legislative session in which your law was passed, then click the House or Senate bill number of your law. This will bring up an extremely useful summary of your law's path through the legislature, detailing sponsors, the dates of the bill's introduction, committee assignments, readings, and roll call votes. There are hyperlinks to Word files of the draft bill and the language of each amendment. By printing this page, and all the linked documents, you will have the basic legislative history of your law.

3. Taped Debates and Committee Meetings

While there are no transcripts of Kentucky debates, for years Kentucky Educational Television (KET) has videotaped the activities of the General Assembly, and the raw footage is available to researchers. The LRC's Legislative Reference Library at the state capitol in Frankfort has videotapes of floor debates dating back to 1992, as well as an eight-year archive of interim committee tapes and a four-year archive of committee meeting tapes.

Floor debate tapes can be viewed at the LRC library or they can be purchased for $10.00 per tape. Not all committee meetings are taped (recording is done at the discretion of the committee chair), so contact the library to see if tapes are available. If tapes exist, they can be viewed at the library or copied for $5.00 a tape. Typed summary minutes of unrecorded committee meetings also can be viewed at the library.

Researchers seeking to buy tapes must be precise as to which tapes they are asking to purchase. Those who decide to view the tapes must do so in Frankfort, so it is advisable to call ahead for details. In either case, it is a good idea to have a detailed chronology of the bill before visiting because the tapes are only organized by date. It goes without saying that a researcher should be prepared to spend some time viewing videotapes.

Recently, KET has been uploading video of legislative activities on its website, with highlights, committee meetings, and floor debates dating back to 2010 now available there (http://www.ket.org/legislature/).

C. Researching External Sources of Legislative History

Because there are so few official print sources to determine legislative intent regarding a law, researchers often turn to less official sources, including LRC staff reports, law review articles, and newspapers reporting on the activities of the legislature.

1. Publications of the Legislative Research Commission

While the Kentucky legislature rarely publishes formal reports, the LRC staff often drafts nonpartisan summaries of issues before the Kentucky General Assembly. Checking the publications of the LRC is a prudent step in legislative research. Note, however, that the LRC is tightly reined in by the General Assembly and, as such, its publications are written in neutral language designed to avoid the appearance of bias to any party. So, even if an LRC publication deals with the topic you are researching, it may not be helpful in elucidating legislative intent.

There are two continuing numbered series published by the LRC, the *Informational Bulletin* and the *Research Reports* series. Two particular publications may be useful: *Issues Confronting the* [year] *General Assembly* (1974–present) and *Mid-interim Reports of the Joint, Special and Statutory Committees* (1973–present). In addition, a number of publications address special topics, ranging from county and municipal law to the Kentucky constitution. The best way to find out if there is an LRC publication on your topic is to search the University of Louisville's online library catalog using your subject of interest as one keyword and "legislative research commission" as another. Current LRC publications are also available as PDFs on its website: Research Reports (http://www.lrc.ky.gov/lrcpubs/research_reports.htm) and Informational Bulletins (http://www.lrc.ky.gov/lrcpubs/info_bulletins.htm).

2. Law Reviews and Bar Publications

Many laws originate as suggestions from the academic community or from leading members of the bar. Often these reformers describe their proposals in state legal periodicals. The easiest way to find these articles is to check the annotations to the KRS section in question in both annotated codes to see if the editors found any secondary sources. To be thorough, also check the two law

Table 6-3. Bill Tracking Overview

1. Go to the Legislative Research Commission website (http://www.lrc.ky.gov).
2. Choose "Legislation" from the top navigation bar.
3. Click the link for the current session, for example, "2016 Regular Session."
4. If you know the bill number, click the "Bills" link. Then, click the number of the bill.
5. When you don't know the bill number or want to research by topic, click the "Bill & Amendment Index—Headings" link. Scan the list of headings to find bills relevant to your research topic. Click all the bill numbers under that heading and read the summaries.

journals with a state focus, the *Kentucky Law Journal* and the *Northern Kentucky Law Review*, and the Kentucky Bar Association's official publication, *Bench & Bar*, indexed in Kentucky Bench & Bar Cumulative Index, 1936–present (https://www.kybar.org/page/bbindex).

3. Newspapers

Newspaper coverage of the General Assembly often provides the best insight into the enactment of a law. Many major Kentucky papers are available on Westlaw or Lexis, including the *Courier-Journal* (LexisNexis 2002–present) and the *Lexington Herald-Leader* (Westlaw 1983–present). Westlaw's Kentucky News database also has coverage dating back to 1990 based on stories from the *Lexington Herald-Leader*, the *Cincinnati Post*, and Associated Press (AP) wires. The *Newsbank* database available at many university and some public law libraries in Kentucky provides full-text access to articles by the Lexington *Herald-Leader* (KY) (1983–present) and many local newspapers and broadcast journalists. Major Kentucky papers also have for-pay archives of back issues available online.

III. Bill Tracking in Kentucky

New legislation can often have an effect on a specific matter that a lawyer is researching or a general area of law that affects the future interests of current or future clients. A lawyer must be able to track the progress of known bills and to search for legislation by topic. See Table 6-3 for a brief overview of the online bill tracking process.

A. Researching by Bill Number

If you know the bill number, tracking legislation is relatively easy on the LRC website (see Table 6-3). In addition, the Bill Status Line (1-866-840-2835) can be consulted to find out where the bill is in the process. Interested parties can also sign up for Bill Watch to receive e-mail notifications of a bill's status.

B. Researching by Topic

Often lawyers want to know if bills are pending on topics affecting their practice. To research by topic, follow the procedure in Table 6-3 to view the list of headings. Peruse these headings carefully. It is also possible to set up a Bill Watch alert, which will send an e-mail when there are developments on any legislation under the topic or topics you choose.

IV. Federal Legislative Research

Researching federal legislation follows some of the same lines as that of Kentucky—but with some significant differences. The U.S. Congress is bigger (100 senators and 435 representatives) and is in continual session, so the scale is larger. In addition, the federal constitution imposes few limits on the number of topics that Congress can address in a single bill, so federal laws generally are more complex. However, there is also richer data available to researchers, including hearings, reports, and floor debates.

An excellent website maintained by the Library of Congress has a storehouse of well-organized federal legislative material. Congress.gov (http://congress.gov) provides bills, bill summaries and status logs, committee reports, and the *Congressional Record*, which records debate in both the House and Senate. Full coverage only goes back to 1989.

A. Federal Legislative History

Researching federal legislative history involves similar steps to researching Kentucky laws, but because Congress publishes hearings, reports, and floor debates, you will encounter more documents (see Table 6-4 for a brief comparison of Kentucky and federal sources for legislative history).

As with Kentucky legislative history, you must begin federal legislative history with a statute citation. With a statute number, you can find the session law ci-

Table 6-4. Comparison of Sources for Kentucky and Federal Legislative History

Action	Kentucky Sources	Federal Sources
Committee work	Minutes, audio tapes available in Frankfort.	Printed committee reports and some hearing transcripts.
Debate in House and Senate	Videotapes available in Frankfort. *Journal of the House* and *Journal of the Senate* record daily activities of Kentucky General Assembly but not the text of the debates.	*Congressional Record* publishes the statements of members of Congress during debate.
Session law	*Kentucky Acts*	*Statutes at Large*
Codified law	Kentucky Revised Statutes	*United States Code*
Publications of codified law	*Michie's Kentucky Revised Statutes* *Baldwin's Kentucky Revised Statutes Annotated*	*United States Code* *United States Code Annotated* *United States Code Service*

tation and public law number, which will lead to the legislative history of the bill as it worked its way through Congress.

When a federal statute is published, it is assigned a public law number. The number is in the form Pub. L. No. 107-110, where the number before the hyphen is the number of the Congress that passed the law and the number after the hyphen is assigned sequentially, based on the order in which the bill was passed. The public law number given above, for example, is for the No Child Left Behind Act of 2001, which was the 110th law signed by the president during the 107th Congress.

The new law is then published as a session law in *United States Statutes at Large*, which is the federal counterpart to *Kentucky Acts*. Session laws are designated by volume and page in *Statutes at Large*, e.g., 215 Stat. 1425. Finally, the new law is assigned a statute number when it is codified with statutes on the same topic in the *United States Code*. For example, the No Child Left Behind Act is codified at 20 U.S.C. §§6301–7941.

1. Sources of Federal Legislative History

The goal of federal legislative history research is to find committee reports, committee hearings, and transcripts of floor debates. Committee reports are considered the most persuasive authority. Unlike the Kentucky General Assembly, Congress publishes lengthy documents detailing committee actions.

Table 6-5. Selected Resources for Federal Legislative History

Resources	Contents
United States Code Congressional and Administrative News (USCCAN)	Selected reprints and excerpts of the most important committee reports, tables showing other reports, and the days where floor debate can be found in the *Congressional Record*.
Congressional Information Service (CIS)	Full text of bills, committee reports, and hearings on microfiche; print indexes and abstracts; online service CIS Congressional Universe increasingly mirrors microfilm and print materials.
Congressional Record	Debate from the floor of Congress.

These reports contain the committee's analysis of the bill, the reasons for enacting it, and often the views of those who disagree with those reasons. Congressional hearings include transcripts of testimony and supporting documents.

Floor debates are published in the *Congressional Record*. Be wary of relying on these debates as they may not have been delivered in that format; members of Congress can amend their remarks and submit remarks after the fact. Moreover, courts are aware that some members try to use floor remarks to influence the interpretations of future judges by reading meaning into the legislation under discussion that they could not get into the actual language of the bill.

2. Print Resources for Federal Legislative History

Table 6-5 contains the most important print sources for researching federal legislative history.

3. Online Resources for Federal Legislative History

Congress.gov (http://congress.gov), official website of the federal legislative branch, provides bill summaries and status, committee reports, and the *Congressional Record*. The Government Publishing Office's govinfo website (http://www.govinfo.gov) contains bills, selected hearings and reports, and the *United States Code*. Much federal legislative history is available on Lexis and Westlaw, although for recent years those services do little to supplement the free government databases.

4. Compiled Legislative History

Some researchers have compiled legislative history for certain federal statutes. Nancy P. Johnson's *Sources of Compiled Legislative Histories* (AALL, 1979–present) indexes all major compilations of federal laws. HeinOnline (http://www.heinonline.org) has digital versions of dozens of compiled legislative histories, as well as an online version of Johnson's index.

B. Federal Bill Tracking

Many of the same sources used for legislative history research are also useful in tracking federal bills that have been introduced but not yet enacted. The Congress.gov site is especially effective.

Chapter 7

Administrative Law

Administrative law is primary authority like statutes and cases. Because it often seems less familiar to new researchers, this chapter begins with an introduction to administrative law and its creation, then turns to research techniques and tools.

I. Introduction to Administrative (and Other Executive Branch) Law

Administrative law is made up of the decisions and rules of various governmental agencies. Government agencies are created by the primary law-making body of the government. For example, the Kentucky legislature creates Kentucky state government agencies and the United States Congress creates federal government agencies. Agencies are created to provide rules, often called *regulations*, which the members of the law-making body lack the technical expertise (or often the desire) to create themselves. For example, while some members of Congress may have some knowledge of water pollution causes, they would not be able to create standards for drinking water as effectively as scientists who specialize in water pollution.

To create an agency that will have the expertise necessary to enact technical rules, the legislature must first pass a statute, known as an *enabling act*, which creates the agency and delegates to the agency the power to create rules that will further the intent of the statute. Some functions are viewed as so necessary to a functioning state government that the state constitution serves as the "act" that creates the agency. For example, section 91 of the Kentucky constitution creates the office of the commissioner of agriculture, the secretary of state, and the attorney general, among others. All of these officers serve as the head of an administrative agency. Most enabling acts allow the agency to create technical rules necessary to enforce statutes; they also give the agency broad powers to internally adjudicate violations of those rules. Agencies, however, are limited by the power delegated to them through the legislature and may not pass rules or adjudicate any cases not covered by the enabling act.

While agencies are created by the legislative branch, their function is to enforce the law, which is an executive branch function. Since they are given enforcement powers, agencies, once created, normally become part of the executive branch. The rules created by these administrative agencies read much like statutes and are considered to be primary authority just like cases and statutes. While adjudicative decisions of agencies have the force of law, they are often challenged in the court systems of the jurisdictions in which the agency is located.

In addition to administrative agencies, the executive branch has one additional individual with the power to create primary authority. This individual is the head of the executive branch. In Kentucky and other states, the head of the executive branch is the governor. In the federal system, the head of the executive branch is the President of the United States. The head of the executive branch has the power to issue new orders and proclamations on his or her own authority, pardon individuals, reorganize executive departments, and make appointments, as well as several other powers. Whenever the head of the executive branch exercises these powers, the document created has the same effect as documents issued from agencies.

II. How Do Kentucky Agencies Create Administrative Law?

In Kentucky, once an agency is created, it must follow a specific set of guidelines and procedures in order to have regulations promulgated (the term for "passing" or "enacting" a regulation). These guidelines are contained in Chapter 13A of the Kentucky Revised Statutes. Kentucky allows two types of administrative regulations, ordinary regulations and emergency regulations. The type of regulation determines the process the agency is required to use when promulgating the regulation as well as the effective date of the regulation and how long the regulation will be effective.

Ordinary regulations have a very specific process they must follow in order to become effective under the Kentucky Revised Statutes. The first requirement for a new proposed regulation is that it be published in the monthly publication *Administrative Register of Kentucky*. Also required are notification of the date, time, and location of public hearings on the regulation, an indication of the manner by which written comments are to be submitted and the deadline for submitting any comments. After holding a public hearing and allowing for written comments to the proposed regulation, the agency is then required to produce a written document, called a *statement of consideration*, showing each comment received and providing the agency's response to each comment. This document, along with a copy of the proposed regulation, is then sent to the compiler of regulations. This portion of the process is similar to that used by the federal government and several other states. Kentucky adds two additional steps before a regulation can become effective.

Kentucky requires that any proposed regulation be reviewed by two different standing subcommittees of the Kentucky legislature. The first subcommittee, the Administrative Regulation Review Subcommittee, reviews proposed regulations (and their supporting documents) for compliance with the provisions of Chapter 13A of the Kentucky Revised Statutes. After the technical review is completed, the proposed regulation then goes to a second committee, which reviews the subject matter covered by the regulation. This "subject matter" subcommittee conducts a review of the proposed regulation to insure that the agency has actually been given the statutory power to issue regulations covering the particular subject.

Either subcommittee may issue a finding that the proposed regulation is deficient. A finding of deficiency, however, does not mean that the regulation cannot take effect. In fact, the Kentucky Supreme Court has found that any attempt by the legislature to veto regulations is an unconstitutional violation of the separation of powers.[1] To avoid this separation of powers problem, the findings of deficiency are deemed to be nonbinding and a regulation found to be deficient can be approved by the governor and go into effect notwithstanding the finding of deficiency. While it is possible for a regulation to go into effect after a finding of deficiency, this is not a common occurrence (although it can happen if the governor approves the regulation despite the deficiencies). While the finding is not binding on an agency, if the regulation is challenged in court, the Kentucky courts are free, but not required, to use the finding of deficiency to determine that the regulation violates the statutes governing promulgation of regulations. If the regulation is not found to be deficient or if the deficiencies are corrected, the regulation goes into effect 30 days after the review by the second subcommittee is completed.

The other type of regulations promulgated in Kentucky, emergency regulations, can potentially bypass some of this process. Emergency regulations can only be issued in four instances: 1) To meet an imminent threat to public safety, health,

1. *Legis. Research Comm. ex rel. Prather v. Brown*, 664 S.W.2d 907, 919 (Ky. 1984).

or welfare; 2) To prevent a loss of federal or state funds; 3) To meet federal or state deadlines; or 4) To protect human health or the environment.

An emergency regulation takes effect immediately upon being filed with the compiler of regulations, but only remains in effect for 180 days. The agency filing the emergency regulation can choose whether it wishes the regulation to only be effective for the 180-day period or whether the regulation will be replaced by a permanent regulation as soon as practical. The agency must identify whether the emergency regulation will be replaced when it files the regulation. Emergency regulations that will not be replaced by an ordinary regulation must follow the same procedure outlined above. Emergency regulations that will be replaced by an ordinary regulation are not required to have a public comment period or a hearing. They are also allowed to take effect before being reviewed by the legislative subcommittees (although a review is still conducted).

III. Researching Kentucky Administrative Law

A. Finding Kentucky Regulations

Kentucky regulations can be located in two related publications. These are the *Kentucky Administrative Regulations Service* and the *Administrative Register of Kentucky*. The *Kentucky Administrative Regulations Service* (or KAR) is the official compilation of Kentucky regulations. It is published each year, usually around late August or early September, and includes all regulations in effect as of June fifteenth of that year.[2] Regulations that were not yet in effect as of June fifteenth or changes to regulations that occurred after June fifteenth can be located using the *Administrative Register of Kentucky*. The *Administrative Register* is published each month on the first of the month and contains not only proposed regulations and notices of hearings (see above), but also contains the text of all regulations which became effective since the first of the prior month. Unofficial copies of both the *Kentucky Administrative Regulations* and the current issue of the *Administrative Register* are available on the Kentucky Legislative Re-

2. Since 2007, the *Kentucky Administrative Regulations* has included all regulations in effect as of June fifteenth of the year. The 2004, 2005, and 2006 editions included all regulations in effect as of July fifteenth. From 1988 to 2003, the *Kentucky Administrative Regulations* included all regulations in effect as of August fifteenth. Prior to 1987, the *Kentucky Administrative Regulations* included all regulations in effect as of the first Monday in July. While the *Kentucky Administrative Regulations* is published each year, there is no statute or regulation that specifies that it must be released each year or that specifies a cut-off date after which regulations will not be included.

search Commission's website (http://www.lrc.ky.gov/kar/frntpage.htm). Although unofficial, the web version of the *Kentucky Administrative Regulations* incorporates changes as of the fifteenth of every month, making it the most up to date version of the *Kentucky Administrative Regulations.* Bloomberg Law, Lexis Advance, and Westlaw all have electronic versions of the *Kentucky Administrative Regulations* available. All three services update their versions of the *Kentucky Administrative Regulations* as of the fifteenth of each month.

Relevant Kentucky regulations can be identified using a variety of methods. First, you can obtain a citation from another source such as a journal article or a judicial opinion. Second, you can research regulations in the *Kentucky Administrative Regulations* by searching for the agency that issued them. Third, you can identify pertinent regulations by researching the topic. Finally, you can find regulations by checking specific statutes to determine if agency regulations exist under those statutes. Each of these methods requires a slightly different approach, which is explained below.

1. Finding a Regulation with a Citation

Finding a regulation by citation is fairly straightforward. The citation style preferred by the *Kentucky Administrative Regulations* is [title number] KAR [chapter number] : [number of specific regulation], for example, 403 KAR 25:130. Citations appearing in law journals use the abbreviation "Ky. Admin. Regs." to identify the *Kentucky Administrative Regulations Service,* but the numbers used in the citation are still the same.

Citations to regulations that are not yet incorporated into the *Kentucky Administrative Regulations* when a case or article is published will cite to the *Administrative Register.* Citations to the *Administrative Register* are to volume number and page number and can appear in three formats: 1) Volume 34, Kentucky Register, page 410; 2) 34 Ky. R. 410; or 3) 34 Ky. Admin. Reg. 410 (Aug. 2007), depending on the source of the citation. The volume number is the number of years since publication of the *Administrative Register* began in 1974. A new volume begins each year with the July issue.[3] Page numbers run consecutively from the July issue through the following year's June issue.

2. Researching by Agency

Regulations can also be located in the *Kentucky Administrative Regulations* through another simple procedure if you know the agency that issued the reg-

---

3. Prior to 1981, new volumes began with the August issue and ended with the July issue.

ulation. The *Kentucky Administrative Regulations* is actually organized by administrative agency. Each volume of the *Kentucky Administrative Regulations* includes a "Table of Titles and Chapters," which identifies where each agency's regulations appear.

3. Searching by Topic

To assist researchers in locating information by topic, each edition of the *Kentucky Administrative Regulations* has a subject, or general, index at the end of the final volume of the set. Three different indexes appear at the back of the last volume, all on colored paper (the color of the paper changes from year to year). Frequently, the paper color used for the general index differs from the paper color used for the other indexes.

4. Finding Regulations Related to Particular Statutes

As explained at the beginning of this chapter, regulations cannot exist without a statute that authorizes their existence. In addition to these enabling acts, regulations frequently have several other statutes to which they relate.

There are two ways through which regulations that deal with a particular statute can be located. The most common way is through the "KRS Index" that appears in the back of the final volume of the *Kentucky Administrative Regulations*. This index lists all Kentucky statutes (in order by number) with the regulations related to the subject covered by the statute. The other way to determine whether a statute has a related regulation is to look up the statute in *Baldwin's Kentucky Revised Statutes*. *Baldwin's* includes "Kentucky Administrative Code References" after each statute (if there is a regulation related to that particular statute). Note that *Michie's Kentucky Revised Statutes*, Kentucky's other official statutory compilation, does not include references to the *Kentucky Administrative Regulations*.

5. Finding Older Regulations

Occasionally, it is necessary to locate an older version of a regulation. This can be necessary if a regulation has recently changed or a client has something that was "grandfathered" in under the rules of an older regulation. A classic example of this situation is building codes. As long as there have been no major renovations to a building, the building only has to conform to standards in effect when the building was constructed. This can impact such things as electrical standards, plumbing standards, and handicapped access as well as a host of other issues. Just as with all areas of law, there are exceptions, but for the most part the older regulations would control.

In order to find an older version of a regulation, the first step is to determine when the regulation changed. Following each regulation in the *Kentucky Administrative Regulations* is a parenthetical showing when that regulation was first promulgated, when each change to the regulation occurred, and where changes can be located in the *Administrative Register*. For example, the parenthetical following 806 KAR 9:060 reads as follows: (I-9.08, 1 Ky.R. 861; eff. 5-14-75; Am. 9 Ky.R. 611, 779; eff. 12-1-82; 27 Ky.R. 1335, 1804; eff. 1-15-2001; TAm eff. 8-9-2007; 37 Ky.R. 972; eff. 11-05-2010). This information shows that 806 KAR 9:060 was amended twice in both 1982 and 2001 and once in 2010. There was also a temporary amendment which took effect in 2007. *Administrative Register* cites for temporary regulations are not included in the parenthetical, but the text of those changes can be located using the index in the *Administrative Register* from the year in which the temporary amendment occurred.

The first entry in the parenthetical (in this instance the first two entries) shows when the regulation was first promulgated. Regulations that were first promulgated in or after 1975 will have a citation to the *Administrative Register* showing where the original regulation can be found and the date for which it was effective. Regulations which were first promulgated prior to 1975 (such as this one) will have two entries showing where they first appeared. The first entry (I-9.08 for this regulation) shows that this regulation came from the pre-1975 version of the *Kentucky Administrative Regulations Service*. In 1974, the Kentucky legislature passed Senate Bill 172 which created the form of the *Kentucky Administrative Regulations* that is still in use today.[4] Prior to 1975, each agency's regulations were numbered separately. The "I" in the citation above showed that it was a Department of Insurance regulation and the 9.08 was their regulation number. Senate Bill 172 called for all regulations to be re-numbered in the title: chapter: section format that is still used. Senate Bill 172 also required each regulation an agency wanted to remain in effect to be resubmitted to the Legislative Research Commission prior to July 1, 1975. Each resubmitted regulation was recorded in the first volume of the *Administrative Register*, and officially retook effect in 1975.

To locate the older versions of a regulation, you may either locate the edition of the *Kentucky Administrative Regulations* from the year before each change or locate the *Administrative Register* where the change was published, depending on which is easier to locate. The University of Louisville Law Library has

---

4. Senate Bill 172 became part of KRS Chapter 13, which was repealed in 1984 and replaced with KRS Chapter 13A which remains in effect. Current rules relating to the formatting of regulations appear in Chapter 13A.

a complete collection of both the *Kentucky Administrative Regulations* and the *Administrative Register* from 1974 to the present. Other law libraries in Kentucky have substantial collections of prior editions as well. When a regulation is amended in the *Administrative Register*, removed wording is bolded, italicized, and struck through. Added or changed wording is bolded, italicized, and underlined.

Locating changes to regulations prior to 1975 is much more difficult. In 1949, a single volume was published containing all regulations then in effect. A second edition was published in 1951. From 1952 to 1958, all new and changed regulations were collected by the Statute Revision Commission (now the Legislative Research Commission), and may still be available in their archives and may, in certain instances, be available from the agencies themselves. Often these older regulations have been destroyed or shipped to the state archives. No attempt was made to print these regulations in any collected format. From 1958 to 1974, Kentucky regulations were published in a loose-leaf format. When a regulation was changed, the pages containing that regulation were removed and replaced with pages containing the new regulation. The University of Louisville Law Library has two copies of this loose-leaf service, one which was last updated in 1971 and one with regulations through 1974. It is possible that the University of Kentucky Law Library, the State Law Library, or the Kentucky Department of Libraries and Archives may also possess copies of this loose-leaf service. As with regulations which were added or changed from 1952–1958, the only possible places copies of regulations changed between 1958–1970 may be available is in the archives of the Legislative Research Commission or the archives of the individual agency.

6. Incorporation by Reference

Users of the *Kentucky Administrative Regulations* and *Administrative Register of Kentucky* frequently find references to documents which have been incorporated into a regulation by reference. These documents are often manuals, federal guidelines, forms, or institutional policies, but can be other types of documents. It can be very frustrating to search for an agency's rules on a subject, only to find that the policy comes from an external document. Occasionally, a Google search will locate the document, but often other methods are required to obtain the document.

Any agency that incorporates a document by reference into the *Kentucky Administrative Regulations* must submit a copy of that document to the Legislative Research Commission. Agencies are also supposed to submit a new copy each time the document changes. These documents are made available to the public via the Legislative Research Commission's reading room. Agencies which incorporate a document by reference are also required to retain a copy of that document and make it available to any member of the public that requests it.

B. Researching the Enabling Act(s)

When researching regulations, the first question to ask is whether the agency acted within its power. If that is in doubt, the first step in challenging the regulation is to locate the statute (or constitutional provision) that gave the agency the power to create the regulation. Kentucky law requires that all regulations include, at the beginning of the regulation, a list of Kentucky statutes, or constitutional provisions, federal statutes, and federal regulations related to the subject covered by the regulation. Immediately after the list of material related to the subject matter of the regulation, the agency promulgating the regulation is required to list the statutes it believes confers on the agency the right to create the regulation. This makes locating the enabling act(s) a simple process once the regulation has been located.

Once the statutory authority of the regulation has been identified, the next step is to locate cases that have interpreted the statute's provisions. Chapter 5 discusses the process of using *Michie's Kentucky Revised Statutes* and *Baldwin's Kentucky Revised Statutes* to find statutes, while Chapter 2 discusses the methods by which individuals can locate provisions of the Kentucky constitution. The annotations in either set of the Kentucky Revised Statutes provide citations to cases that may be relevant to the issue of whether the agency exceeded its powers. It may also be useful to check annotations to specific provisions in KRS Chapter 13A. Chapters 3 and 4 discuss how to locate cases in addition to those found in the annotated codes.

C. Finding Updates to Kentucky Regulations

The *Administrative Register of Kentucky* contains all updates to regulations since the last release of the *Kentucky Administrative Regulations* (the prior June fifteenth). Each monthly issue includes the text of regulations that have been proposed by agencies as well as amendments to regulations that have occurred during the approval process. To determine which of these regulations have become effective, it is necessary to use the "Locator Index-Effective Dates" section of the *Administrative Register*. The Locator Index is the first index that appears in the colored pages at the back of each monthly issue. The Locator Index is arranged by regulation number so it is fairly easy to determine if a specific regulation has been updated. The index is cumulative for the entire volume of the *Administrative Register*, meaning that any regulation updated since the July issue will be identified in the index of the most recent *Administrative Register*. The index also usually includes some regulations from the prior volume that had not yet gone into effect when the *Kentucky Administrative Regulations* was printed.

Following the entry for the regulation number, a reference is given to the page of the *Administrative Register* where the change was published. Effective dates are included for any changes which had taken effect as of the publication date of that issue. Not all changes to regulations appear in this index. Only changes that were requested by the agency appear in the Locator Index. Changes made to regulations by the publishing staff in order to correct errors or changes to the name of an administrative body appear in the "Technical Amendment Index."

There are two additional indexes that can be used to find regulations that have changed. The "KRS Index" performs a function similar to the "KRS Index" in the *Kentucky Administrative Regulations*. It provides a listing of any statute which appears in the "relates to" portion of a regulation; however, the *Administrative Register*'s version of the index only includes statutes appearing in the "relates to" section of regulations that have appeared in the current volume of the *Administrative Register* (i.e., regulations taking effect after June fifteenth).

The final cumulative index included in the *Administrative Register* purports to be a subject index. In reality, it is an index by administrative body only. It lists, by administrative body, regulations that have become effective since the June fifteenth *Kentucky Administrative Regulations* cutoff date.

Once the text of the amendment is located in the *Administrative Register*, changes are easy to identify. When a regulation is amended in the *Administrative Register*, removed wording is bolded, italicized, and struck through. Added or changed wording is bolded, italicized, and underlined.

IV. Researching Agency Decisions

In addition to their regulation-making functions, administrative agencies also act in a quasi-judicial role, adjudicating cases pertaining to agency rules or actions. There may be several levels of review. The first level of review usually involves a reviewer or hearing officer considering the claimant's file and making a determination. While the majority of agencies are governed by the hearing procedures in Chapter 13B of the Kentucky Revised Statutes, there is no uniform procedure for subsequent reviews due to the significant number of agencies that have been granted an exemption from the requirements. It is advisable to check with the particular agency to determine the appropriate appeals procedure.

If the agency is not included in the list of agencies excluded from the provisions of Chapter 13B, the initial hearing officer is responsible for collecting all of the material from the parties involved and creating a record. Once the parties have had their opportunity to be heard, the hearing officer drafts a recommended order, which is forwarded to the head of the agency and included as part of the record. Either party may file a list of exceptions with the head of the agency. These exceptions are essentially reasons to overturn the hearing officer's decisions. Any exceptions not raised with the head of the agency cannot be used as grounds for a future review by a court.

After reviewing exceptions that have been raised by either party, the head of the agency issues a written final order. The final order may be appealed to the circuit court (usually the Franklin Circuit Court in Frankfort) within 30 days of receipt. Agencies not covered by Chapter 13B have their own procedures for initial review and subsequent reviews. These procedures differ widely, but can be located using either the Kentucky Revised Statutes or the *Kentucky Administrative Regulations.* Regardless of the procedure used, most agencies are required to allow access to agency hearing records under Kentucky's "open records" laws.

Some agency decisions are widely available, such as those from the Kentucky Board of Tax Appeals or the Kentucky Executive Branch Ethics Commission, which appear in print and in several electronic formats. Decisions of other agencies may be available in print, on the agency's website, or from an electronic pay service (or any combination of the three). Westlaw and Lexis have decisions from several Kentucky agencies available as part of their subscriptions.

Administrative agencies are also frequently called upon to provide advice regarding their regulations. Where it is not clear whether certain activities are permitted or prohibited under regulations issued by the agency, an individual or a corporation may submit a request to the agency for guidance. This guidance comes in such forms as Advisory Opinions, Technical Standards, or Guidance Manuals. These materials do not have the same force of law as regulations or adjudications and are not technically legally binding, but they do indicate the intention of the agency to apply statutes and regulations in the manner described in the document. Failure to follow the guidance given in the document could bring civil or criminal penalties both on the entity that requested the guidance and entities facing the same issue in the future. Thus, although they may not be legally binding, reviewing agency materials designed to give guidance can be as important as reviewing any other type of legal materials. For assistance in locating materials for a specific agency, see William A. Hilyerd's *Kentucky Administrative Law Resource Guide* CD-ROM (Office of Continuing Legal Education, University of Kentucky College of Law 2009).

V. Researching Other Executive Materials

A. Attorney General Opinions

The attorney general is the primary lawyer for the Commonwealth of Kentucky. The office of the attorney general in Kentucky was created by the Kentucky constitution. The duties of the attorney general include being the chief law officer for the commonwealth, being the advisor for all governmental bodies, and appearing before the courts in all cases in which the commonwealth has an interest (including all criminal cases).

As part of these duties, the attorney general is required to issue written opinions, if requested to do so, on any legal issue that arises in any governmental body as part of that body's official duties. The attorney general may also issue an opinion without being requested to do so if he or she deems that the subject matter covered would make having an official opinion desirable. The attorney general is also responsible for issuing separate opinions to determine whether agency documents and hearings are required to be available to the public. An opinion of the attorney general is a legally binding precedent unless overturned by a court, and, for some legal issues, an attorney general opinion is the only Kentucky law on the subject.

The attorney general's office has existed in Kentucky and has been required to give written opinions to certain government offices since 1799. Opinions from the attorney general were not easily available until the first printed volume of selected opinions appeared in 1908. This volume arranged the selected opinions by subject matter. Volumes containing selected opinions continued to be published until 1915, with volumes being released every other year. These volumes followed the subject matter arrangement used in the 1908 volume. No printed volumes containing opinions of the attorney general appeared from 1916 to 1927.

A second series was attempted in 1928 and lasted until 1930. This series was also arranged by subject and contained only a portion of the opinions issued during the time period. The 1929–1930 edition was the first to include a subject index. Sequential numbering of opinions began in the 1928 edition (a practice that would continue until 1960). The series disappeared after the 1930 edition and attorney generals' opinions would not be distributed to the public in bound form until the publication of the 1956–1960 collection in 1960. The 1956–1960 volume followed the format of the prior series. Opinions were listed by subject and only a small portion of the issued opinions were included.

In 1960, the Banks-Baldwin company began its publication of the series *Opinions of the Attorney General of Kentucky*, which continues to this day (now published by Thomson Reuters). As with prior editions, only certain opinions were included. In a major departure from prior editions, opinions were printed in order by their opinion numbers instead of being arranged by subject. The numbering system for opinions was also changed. The new numbering system consisted of the two digit year followed by a dash and second number. The second number still represented sequential numbering of opinions, but this second number was now reset at the beginning of each year. Thus, the first opinion issued in 1960 would be 60-1, the second 60-2, while the first opinion issued in 1961 would be 61-1. This numbering system is still in use. Decisions by the attorney general on open records and open meetings laws began appearing in *Opinions of the Attorney General of Kentucky* as of 1992. Also beginning in 1992, the attorney general's office made opinions available via its website (http://ag.ky.gov/civil/civil-enviro/opinions/Pages/default.aspx). While the printed edition still contains selected opinions, the website contains all opinions issued by the attorney general's office since 1992. Open records and open meetings decisions since 1993 are also available via the attorney general's website at http://ag.ky.gov/civil/civil-enviro/orom/Pages/default.aspx.

There are several ways to locate attorney general's opinions on a given subject. Each volume issued since 1929 includes a subject index at the back of the volume. In addition to these volume-by-volume indexes, consolidated indexes exist for the periods 1956–1968, 1968–1979, and 1980–1989. While these indexes can be useful, the most common way of locating attorney general's opinions is through the use of the Kentucky Revised Statutes. Both *Baldwin's Kentucky Revised Statutes Annotated* and *Michie's Kentucky Revised Statutes* include attorney general's opinions as part of their case annotations following each statute. Opinions, open records, and open meetings decisions appearing on the attorney general's webpage can be searched using the search engine built into that page. Lexis Advance and Westlaw have attorney general's opinions from the mid-1970s to the present available on their services.

B. Gubernatorial Materials

The governor of the Commonwealth of Kentucky has the power to issue several types of documents under his or her own authority. Among these documents are executive orders, proclamations, pardons, and reorganization plans. These documents can have a profound effect on the operation of Kentucky government, but they can be notoriously difficult for an inexperienced researcher to locate.

Official acts of the governor are included in a single publication, known as either the *Governor's Journal* or the *Executive Journal*. Actions of the governor are filed in date order in this journal and are indexed by subject. The difficulty in using this journal is that the Kentucky secretary of state maintains the only copy. Selected materials from the journal for the Fletcher, Beshear, and Bevin administrations are available through the Secretary of State's webpage (http://www.sos.ky.gov/admin/Executive/ExecJournal/Pages/default.aspx). For material not available on the webpage, it is necessary to contact the Secretary of State's office and request assistance. Any material that dates before 1927 has been transferred to the Kentucky Department of Libraries and Archives.

VI. Other Resources

The most valuable resource in administrative law research is the agency itself. While statutes and rules are relatively easy to find, other documents such as policies, guidelines, and internal operating documents can be difficult to locate. This is especially true in the case of regulations that have incorporated other documents by reference. The value of contacting a representative of the agency for assistance in locating information cannot be ignored. In addition, many agencies make materials, such as handbooks and procedures for interacting with that agency, available via their websites.

There are some useful general materials for researching administrative law in Kentucky. Some of the most helpful are *Kentucky Administrative Regulations* (Legislative Research Commission Informational Bulletin #118, 2003) which is available both in print and as a PDF download from the Legislative Research Commission (http://www.lrc.ky.gov/lrcpubs/Ib118.pdf),[5] *Kentucky Administrative Law* (2d ed., Office of Continuing Legal Education, University of Kentucky College of Law 2006), and Mathew L. Mooney, *Kentucky Administrative Procedures Act: KRS 13B Annotated* (Office of Continuing Legal Education, University of Kentucky College of Law 2000).

---

5. This publication is no longer listed as available on the Legislative Research Commission's publications page, but the direct link still works.

VII. Researching Federal Administrative Law[6]

The federal government's agencies function much like Kentucky's. Agencies such as the Social Security Administration, the Internal Revenue Service, and the U.S. Fish and Wildlife Service are invaluable parts of the executive branch.

The federal statute that governs the creation of regulations and the conduct of hearings by agencies of the federal government is called the Administrative Procedure Act. Like Chapter 13A of the Kentucky Revised Statutes, the goals of the Administrative Procedure Act are to promote openness in the system, encourage public participation, and grant the public confidence in the fairness of the procedures used by federal government agencies.

A. *Code of Federal Regulations*

Just like the rules created by Kentucky agencies, rules created by federal government agencies are called regulations. Federal regulations are published by the U.S. Government Publishing Office in the *Code of Federal Regulations* (CFR).

Similar to the *Kentucky Administrative Regulations* in Kentucky, regulations in the CFR are organized by agency and subject. The 50 titles of the CFR do not necessarily correspond to the 54 titles of the *United States Code* (USC), although some topics do fall under the same title number. For instance, Title 7 in both the CFR and the USC pertain to agriculture, but Title 11 of the USC addresses bankruptcy, while the same title in the CFR deals with federal elections.

CFR volumes are updated annually, with specific titles updated each quarter. Titles 1, 2, and 4 through 16 are updated as of January 1; Titles 17 through 27 are updated as of April 1; Titles 28 through 41 are updated as of July 1; and Titles 42 through 50 are updated as of October 1. Title 3, which contains presidential documents, is not updated each year per se. It is an annual compilation of all presidential documents released during the prior year. Each year's Title 3 contains completely different documents. Note that the updated date of a title is not always the same as the date when a particular title or volume is released. It is not uncommon for a title or portion of a title to be released in print two to three months (or longer) after its "updated as of" date. Each year, the covers of CFR volumes are a different color, which makes it easy to tell whether a print volume has been updated.

---

6. Portions of this section are drawn from *Oregon Legal Research* by Suzanne E. Rowe and are used with permission.

The most common way to research a topic in the CFR is to use the general index. The index contains both common terms and names of agencies. However, it may be more efficient to begin the research in an annotated statutory code, such as West's *United States Code Annotated* or LexisNexis's *United States Code Service*. After locating a statute on point, review the annotations following the statute for cross-references to relevant regulations. The *United States Code Service* tends to provide more references to regulations than does the *United States Code Annotated*.

The CFR is also available via commercial electronic research services such as Lexis Advance and Westlaw, and is available free of charge on the Internet from the U.S. Government Publishing Office's govinfo website (https://govinfo.gov/). Using one of these electronic versions may be more efficient than using the CFR in print. The sites not only allow searching by keyword, but also incorporate changes to the regulations much more frequently than does the print version. (Revisions are usually included within a week of the change.) The quick incorporation of changes eliminates the need to update regulations. Chapter 11 details some of the locations where online access to the CFR can be found and the most effective way to use the various electronic services. Updating procedures for the print edition are described below for users of the print version.

B. *Federal Register*

New regulations and proposed changes to existing regulations are published first in the *Federal Register*, the federal equivalent of the *Administrative Register of Kentucky*. The *Federal Register* is published daily (except weekends and holidays), with continuous pagination throughout the year. This means that page numbers in the tens of thousands are common. In addition to new and proposed regulations, the *Federal Register* is the official source for notices of hearings and responses to comments on proposed regulations. Like the CFR, the *Federal Register* is available from a variety of electronic sources as well as in print. For information on the electronic sources, please see Chapter 11.

C. Updating Federal Regulations

The process of updating a federal regulation begins with a small publication called the *List of Sections Affected*. The *List of Sections Affected* can be found in print or on the Government Publishing Office's govinfo website. As its name suggests, the *List of Sections Affected* lists all sections of the CFR that have been affected by recent agency action. The *List of Sections Affected* also provides page references to *Federal Register* issues where action affecting a section of the CFR is included. If a section is not listed in the *List of Sections Affected*, then it has not been changed since its annual revision. The *List of Sections Affected* is published monthly, allowing a user to update a regulation through the end of the month listed on the cover of the publication.

Final updating requires referencing a table in the back of the *Federal Register* called "CFR Parts Affected During [the current month]." Do not confuse this table with the "CFR Parts Affected in This Issue" table located in the contents at the beginning of each issue. Refer to this table in each *Federal Register* for the last day of each month for all of the months between the most recent *List of Sections Affected* issue and the current date. Also, check the most recent issue of the *Federal Register* for the present month. The table contains more general information than does the *List of Sections Affected* (it only tells if a part has been modified, while the *List of Sections Affected* indicates which sections within a particular part have changed), but will note changes made since the most recent *List of Sections Affected.*

The updating described above is similar to updating using pocket parts. Federal regulations can be Shepardized using Lexis Advance or can be updated with KeyCite on Westlaw. (See Chapter 9 for more information.)

D. Researching Decisions of Federal Agencies

Like Kentucky agencies, federal agencies hold quasi-judicial hearings to decide cases that arise under the agency's regulations. Some of these decisions are published in reporters specific to each agency, for example, *Decisions and Orders of the National Labor Relations Board.* A list of selected federal agency reporters is available in Appendix 7(A) to the fifth edition of the *ALWD Guide to Legal Citation.* A slightly different list appears as Table T1.2 in the current (twentieth) edition of *The Bluebook.*

E. Judicial Opinions

The methods of case research explained in Chapters 3 and 4 will lead to opinions in which the judiciary reviewed decisions of federal agencies. Additionally, Shepard's on Lexis Advance, KeyCite on Westlaw, and BCite on Bloomberg Law (see Chapter 9) are useful research tools both for updating federal regulations and for finding cases relevant to regulatory research.

Chapter 8

Court Rules and Ethics

I. Introduction to Court Rules

Court rules govern litigation practice from the filing of the initial pleadings through the final appeal. Court rules can dictate details ranging from the size of paper to be used in court filings to the proper ethical behavior of attorneys and judges. The Kentucky constitution gives the Kentucky Supreme Court the authority to create rules governing the operation of Kentucky courts.[1] The Kentucky Supreme Court has collected the rules it has promulgated into seven areas: Rules of Civil Procedure, Rules of Criminal Procedure, Rules of Evidence, Family court rules, Juvenile court rules, Supreme Court Rules, and Administrative Procedures of the Court of Justice. In addition to these rules, the Supreme Court has authorized the chief judge of each of the 57 judicial circuits and 60 judicial districts in Kentucky to promulgate rules that allow for the orderly operation of the courts in that circuit or district.[2] Many circuits and districts have also created rules governing operation of their special courts, such as family courts.

II. Researching Kentucky Rules

A. Sources of Rules

Court rules in Kentucky can be located in a variety of places. Both LexisNexis and Thomson Reuters' West Publishing division publish special sets containing the entire text of the statewide rules (i.e., the Rules of Civil Procedure, Rules of Criminal Procedure, Rules of Evidence, Supreme Court Rules, and Administrative Rules of the Court of Justice). The LexisNexis version, *Michie's Kentucky Revised Statutes: Kentucky Rules Annotated* volumes 1 and 2, provides not only the text of the rules, but also a listing of cases and secondary sources that

---

1. Ky. Const. § 116.
2. Ky. Sup. Ct. R. 1.040(a); Ky. R. Civ. P. 13.02.

discuss that particular rule. West's *Kentucky Rules of Court* contains only the text of the rules. West includes an annotated version of the rules as part of *Baldwin's Kentucky Revised Statutes Annotated.* Annotated versions of all of the statewide rules can be located in volumes 34 to 36. West's *Kentucky Rules of Court* appears in full on Westlaw, while *Michie's Kentucky Revised Statutes: Kentucky Rules Annotated* appears in full on Lexis. Full versions of the statewide rules can also be located on the Internet (https://govt.westlaw.com/kyrules/).

Local rules and special court rules, such as those for family courts, can be slightly harder to locate, depending on the circuit or district. To make finding local rules even more difficult, some circuits and districts have not created local rules, so part of the challenge is determining whether rules for a specific court do not exist or the source does not include the needed rules.

The single best place to locate local rules for Kentucky courts is the website of the Kentucky Court of Justice (the umbrella organization for the judicial branch in Kentucky). The court has a webpage (http://courts.ky.gov/Pages/localrules.aspx), which collects all of the local rules. In addition to circuit, district, and family court rules, the website collects other court rules used in local courts such as domestic violence protocols, pretrial diversion rules, and mediation rules. Very few of these additional materials can be found through any other source.

Some local rules can also be found in print collections. The West publication *Kentucky Rules of Court,* volume 3 contains local rules for selected circuit, district, and family courts. The rules for 52 of Kentucky's 57 circuit courts are included in this volume. However, this set contains rules from only 37 of Kentucky's 60 district courts. Rules for 41 of the 43 Kentucky family courts are also included.[3] The LexisNexis version, *Michie's Kentucky Revised Statutes: Kentucky Rules Annotated,* volume 3, contains a similar selection of local rules with rules from 50 circuit courts, 34 district courts, and 38 family courts included. If you cannot locate the local rules you seek in one set, it may be advisable to check the other set. The West version of the local rules contains rules for three circuits, seven districts, and six family courts which are not contained in the LexisNexis version. On the other hand, the LexisNexis version contains rules for one circuit, four districts, and one family court not contained in the West version.[4] For four judicial circuit courts and five district courts, the only access to local rules comes

---

3. There are 36 family courts covering 37 judicial circuits. An additional seven circuits have a family court system that is not included in the 36 recognized family courts.

4. This information is based on a review of the 2017 edition of *Kentucky Rules of Court,* vol. 3 (Thomson Reuters 2017) and the 2017 edition of *Michie's Kentucky Revised Statutes: Kentucky Rules Annotated,* vol. 3 (Lexis-Nexis 2017).

from the Court of Justice's website mentioned above. Ten Kentucky district courts do not have their rules available in either a mass market print source or via the Internet. The rules for the 6th and 53rd circuit's family courts are the only family court rules that are not available through either of the two print sources. The rules for both of these family courts are also not available on the Court of Justice's webpage.

B. Updating Rules

Just like all other legal materials, the text of court rules changes over time. It is very important to be sure that recent changes to a particular court rule have not been overlooked. Changes to court rules can be located in a variety of sources. With the exception of the online version, the sources of court rules are updated on a yearly basis with either pocket parts (*Baldwin's Kentucky Revised Statutes Annotated*, volumes 34 to 36) or replacement volumes (all other print sources). Each source updates at a different time of the year, so checking the title page of the volume being used to verify the currency of the last update is essential.

Online updates can also be located quite easily. For local rules, the single best place to check is the court's website. Local rules are updated on the webpage as soon as they are approved by the Supreme Court. Updates to statewide rules can also be found on the Court of Justice's website (http://apps.kycourts.net/Supreme/SC_Rules.shtm).

In print, updates (and proposed changes) to statewide rules are published in the *Bench & Bar* (currently titled *B & B—Bench & Bar*), the magazine of the Kentucky Bar Association. Updated and proposed rules which have appeared in the *Bench & Bar* can be located using the online index to the *Bench & Bar* (https://www.kybar.org/page/bbindex). Various indexes cover the *Bench & Bar* from its inception in 1936 through 2016, but all indexes are available via this webpage. Full issues of the *Bench & Bar* from 2007 to the present are also available through the Kentucky Bar Association's website (https://www.kybar.org/page/BB). New rules can also be found in the Interim Update Service to *Baldwin's Kentucky Revised Statutes Annotated*, volumes of *Kentucky Decisions*, and advance sheets of the *SouthWestern Reporter*.

C. Interpreting Procedural Rules

1. Case Law

The meaning of a particular court rule may not always be clear. Like statutes, rules that require clarification become the subject of court cases. Finding these cases can be fairly simple, depending on the sources used to find the text of the rule. Both *Michie's Kentucky Revised Statutes: Kentucky Rules Annotated* and *Baldwin's Kentucky Revised Statutes Annotated* provide a means to locate related cases. After each rule, both services provide a list of the major cases that have discussed that particular rule.

2. Other Resources

Frequently, there are no case law listings to provide help in deciphering an unclear rule. In this instance, it may be helpful to locate secondary sources such as treatises that discuss the particular type of rule. Kentucky has several helpful treatises that give guidance when interpreting a particular rule.

For the Rules of Civil Procedure, the most helpful treatise is Kurt A. Phillips, Jr., David V. Kramer, and David W. Burleigh, *Rules of Civil Procedure Annotated* (6th ed., Thomson West 2005) (volumes 6 and 7 of West's *Kentucky Practice* Series). For criminal procedure rules, really the only helpful treatise is Leslie W. Abramson, *Criminal Practice and Procedure* (5th ed., Thomson Reuters 2010) (*Kentucky Practice* volumes 8 and 9).

The Kentucky Rules of Evidence have the largest number of helpful treatise materials available. Guidance on the rules of evidence can be obtained through any of three helpful treatises: Robert G. Lawson, William S. Cooper, and William H. Fortune, *Kentucky Rules of Evidence* (2d ed., Office of Continuing Legal Education, University of Kentucky College of Law 2002); Robert G. Lawson, *The Kentucky Evidence Law Handbook* (5th ed., LexisNexis 2013); or Richard H. Underwood and Glen Weissenberger, *Kentucky Evidence Courtroom Manual* (2016–2017 ed., LexisNexis 2016).

Numerous books and law journal articles discuss federal rules, if no Kentucky specific material exists to help in the interpretation.

III. Ethics Rules

A. Introduction to Ethics Rules

In addition to having the authority to promulgate rules covering the operation of Kentucky courts, the Kentucky Supreme Court has also been given the exclusive power to regulate members of the bar and the judiciary.[5] In order to effectively regulate the legal profession, the Supreme Court adopted the American Bar Association's Model Rules of Professional Conduct (with some

5. Ky. Const. §§ 116, 121.

variations) as Supreme Court Rule 3.130. Copies of the Supreme Court Rules (including the ethics rules) can be located in both *Michie's Kentucky Revised Statutes: Kentucky Rules Annotated* and *Baldwin's Kentucky Revised Statutes Annotated.* These volumes are replaced with updated editions each year. To locate changes which have occurred since the volumes were released, follow the same procedure for updating other court rules discussed above.

The Supreme Court has delegated the initiation and investigation of disciplinary actions to the Kentucky Bar Association and has even authorized the bar association to carry out certain disciplinary actions without consulting the court.[6] All disciplinary actions of the Kentucky Bar Association are appealable to the Supreme Court. The court has also given the Kentucky Bar Association the authority to answer questions regarding the ethics rules. Attorneys who are unsure whether a certain course of action is permissible under the rules can request the opinion of the Kentucky Bar Association. The bar association, when asked, will issue either a formal or informal advisory opinion indicating its interpretation of the particular rule.

B. Interpreting Ethics Rules

1. Kentucky Bar Association Opinions

Under Kentucky Supreme Court Rule 3.530, any licensed attorney in the Commonwealth of Kentucky may request guidance from the Kentucky Bar Association regarding an ethical rule or whether a certain course of action complies with the ethical rules. The request may be either in writing or by telephone. This service is commonly known as the Ethics Hotline. Requests for ethics guidance are referred to a member of the ethics committee. This committee member provides an answer to the requesting attorney both by telephone and in the form of a written informal ethics opinion. These informal opinions are reviewed by the ethics committee as a whole and any issues addressed that the committee deems to be of significant importance can have a formal ethics opinion released by the committee.

Both informal and formal opinions are advisory only; however, the attorney who requested the informal opinion is not subject to discipline if he or she complies with the informal opinion.[7] Informal opinions are not publicly available, but formal ethics committee opinions are printed in the *Bench & Bar* as they are released. A complete collection of formal ethics opinions is available

---

6. Ky. Sup. Ct. R. 3.140–3.510.
7. Ky. Sup. Ct. R. 3.530.

in electronic format via the Kentucky Bar Association's website (https://www.kybar.org/?page=opinsethics), with a search engine for the opinions available as well. The Kentucky Bar Association also sponsors the University of Kentucky CLE publication, *Kentucky Legal Ethics Deskbook*.[8] The relatively new fifth edition includes all formal ethics opinions released by the Kentucky Bar Association through January 2015 in volume 2. It also includes a comprehensive index to the opinions. Newer opinions are available via the Kentucky Bar Association link listed above. Opinions can also be located in the *Bench & Bar* by using the online indexes, available at: https://www.kybar.org/page/bbindex. Ethics opinions are indexed under the topic "Legal Ethics." Legal Ethics opinions from 1962 to the present are also available on Lexis Advance.

The Kentucky Bar Association also issues opinions regarding what constitutes the unauthorized practice of law in Kentucky. Just like regular ethics opinions, these decisions can be found in print in volume 3 of the *Kentucky Legal Ethics Deskbook*. Like regular opinions, Unauthorized Practice of Law opinions are also available on the Kentucky Bar Association's website. Access to Unauthorized Practice decisions is available via search engine (https://www.kybar.org/?OpinsUnauth).

2. Case Law

While ethics opinions issued by the Kentucky Bar Association can help guide an attorney, they are advisory only. This means that they do not have the force of law. The only entity that can make binding decisions regarding ethical behavior is the Kentucky Supreme Court.

Decisions on ethical matters from the Kentucky Supreme Court can be located using three methods. Since legal ethics are governed by rules in Kentucky, both *Michie's Kentucky Revised Statutes: Kentucky Rules Annotated* and *Baldwin's Kentucky Revised Statutes Annotated* provide a means to locate related cases. After each rule, both services provide a list of the major cases that have discussed that particular rule. This format is the same as that used for other rules in Kentucky. Like other Kentucky decisions, ethics decisions can be located using the *Kentucky Digest 2d*. Ethics decisions are indexed primarily under the "Attorney and Client" digest topic, but they can be found elsewhere in the digest depending on the specific ethical rule in question. Finally, cases can be located using *Shepard's Professional and Judicial Conduct Citations*. This publication is arranged by model rule number (from the American Bar Association's Model Rules of Professional Conduct) and lists cases that have cited each individual rule.

---

8. Todd B. Eberle et al., *Kentucky Legal Ethics Deskbook* (5th ed., Office of Continuing Legal Education. University of Kentucky College of Law 2016).

3. Judicial Ethics Committee Decisions

Judges are also covered by ethics rules. The Kentucky Code of Judicial Conduct follows the text of the Model Code of Judicial Conduct. These rules appear in Kentucky as Supreme Court Rule 4.300. Discipline for failing to follow these rules is imposed by the Kentucky Judicial Conduct Commission, but the commission's actions are reviewable by the Supreme Court.[9]

Judges also have an organization, the Judicial Ethics Committee, that can answer questions about whether certain actions are allowable under the ethics rules. Just like the bar association's ethics committee, the Judicial Ethics Committee issues written formal and informal opinions to help guide judges in making sure their actions comply with the ethics rules.

Judicial ethics rules (along with the ethics rules covering lawyers) can be located in the Supreme Court Rules section of the court rules books listed earlier and are updated in the same method as other court rules. Written formal opinions of the Judicial Ethics Committee have no official place of publication; however, they have been included in volume 3 of the *Kentucky Legal Ethics Deskbook* and appear in the *Bench & Bar.* Opinions can also be located in the *Bench & Bar* by using the online indexes, available at https://www.kybar.org/page/bbindex. Judicial ethics opinions are indexed under the topic "Judicial Ethics." Judicial ethics decisions can also be obtained from both Westlaw and Lexis. Both services have opinions from 1979 to the present.

IV. National Sources of Ethics Materials

Quite often there are no Kentucky materials available to help with the interpretation of ethics rules. If all Kentucky resources have been exhausted, it may be helpful to review material from other jurisdictions, as well as discussions of the American Bar Association's Model Rules on which the Kentucky ethics rules are based.

A. Model Rules

The American Bar Association's Model Rules can be located in a variety of sources and are even available free on the Internet.[10] However, two of the most

9. Ky. Sup. Ct. R. 4.010–4.310.

10. The rules are available on the American Bar Association's website at http://www.americanbar.org/groups/professional_responsibility/publications/model_rules_of_professional_conduct/model_rules_of_professional_conduct_table_of_contents.html.

useful versions of the Model Rules are the *Annotated Model Rules of Professional Conduct* (8th ed., Amer. Bar Assoc. 2015) and the *ABA/BNA Lawyer's Manual on Professional Conduct*. The *Annotated Model Rules of Professional Conduct* gives each rule a good deal of discussion and provides citations to cases that have analyzed that rule. The *Lawyer's Manual of Professional Conduct* comes in three parts: Current Reports, the Reference Manual, and Ethics Opinions. The Current Reports section consists of a bi-weekly newsletter that provides discussion of new court cases and ethics opinions as they are issued and highlights trends in professional responsibility. The Reference Manual covers ethical subjects in detail, giving both discussion and substantial references to cases and ethics opinions. The Ethics Opinions section prints the text of new ethics opinions from all jurisdictions.

B. ABA Ethics Opinions

Like the Kentucky Bar Association, the American Bar Association answers questions relating to interpretation of its Model Rules for ethical conduct. American Bar Association ethics opinions can be either formal or informal. Formal opinions cover "a subject matter of general interest to the bar," while informal opinions respond to "a specific inquiry relating to a particular set of facts."[11] The American Bar Association ceased giving informal opinions as of 1989, but many of the older informal opinions are still valid and still apply to actions of attorneys. Both formal and informal opinions can be located in print. The most convenient source for locating American Bar Association opinions (of both types) is the *ABA/BNA Lawyer's Manual on Professional Conduct*'s Ethics Opinions binders, although the American Bar Association does have its own publication containing all of the text of both types of opinions.

C. Other Materials

Other materials can be useful when researching legal ethics. Perhaps the most influential is the *Restatement of the Law: The Law Governing Lawyers* (3d ed., American Law Institute 2000). The Restatement is a collaboration between academics and practicing attorneys. The Restatement attempts to create a document that expresses the ideal guidelines for ethical behavior. Each section is heavily footnoted and discussed. Restatements do not rise to the level of law,

11. 1 *Informal Ethics Opinions* 2 (Committee on Ethics and Professional Responsibility, American Bar Association 1975).

but due to their thoroughness and in-depth discussion they usually are highly respected materials. *The Law Governing Lawyers* is no exception. There are some major differences between the Model Rules and the Restatement. *Lawyer Law: Comparing the ABA Model Rules of Professional Conduct with the ALI Restatement (Third) of the Law Governing Lawyers* by Thomas D. Morgan[12] compares and contrasts the provisions of each and provides some discussion as to why the differences exist.

In addition to the Restatement, several excellent treatises on the subject of legal ethics can be used to interpret the meaning of a particular ethics rule. Some of the best known are Geoffrey C. Hazard and W. William Hodes's *The Law of Lawyering*[13] and William H. Fortune, Richard H. Underwood & Edward J. Imwinkelried's *Modern Litigation and Professional Responsibility Handbook.*[14]

V. Researching Federal Rules

A. Sources of Rules

Federal court rules, such as the Rules of Civil Procedure, the Rules of Criminal Procedure, and the Rules of Evidence, can be found both on the Internet and in various sources in print. As with Kentucky rules, the most helpful versions of the rules are ones that are annotated. Annotated versions of the federal rules can be located in either of the annotated federal codes, *United States Code Annotated* (U.S.C.A.) or *United States Code Service* (U.S.C.S.). Placement of the rules varies between the two sets. In U.S.C.A., the Rules of Criminal Procedure appear as part of Title 18, while the rest of the rules appear as part of Title 28. In U.S.C.S., the rules are found in special rules volumes following Title 54. Federal court rules are readily available on Westlaw and Lexis Advance. Should the U.S.C.A. or U.S.C.S. not be available, unannotated versions of the rules are available on the Internet. One of the best sites for locating unannotated rules is Cornell's Legal Information Institute (http://www.law.cornell.edu/rules/).

---

12. Thomas D. Morgan, *Lawyer Law: Comparing the ABA Model Rules of Professional Conduct with the ALI Restatement (Third) of the Law Governing Lawyers* (Amer. Bar Assoc. 2005).

13. Geoffrey C. Hazard & W. William Hodes, *The Law of Lawyering* (4th ed., Aspen Law & Business 2015).

14. William H. Fortune, Richard H. Underwood & Edward J. Imwinkelried, *Modern Litigation and Professional Responsibility Handbook* (2d ed., Aspen Law & Business 2000).

Just as in the state system, each federal court typically has its own "local" rules. Often, these local rules can be located via the court's webpage. For example, the rules for the Sixth Circuit Court of Appeals are available at http://www.ca6.uscourts.gov/rules-and-procedures.

B. Interpreting Rules

1. Case Law

Cases relevant to federal rules can be located using the annotated codes or the *Federal Practice Digest.* (See Chapter 4 for more information on using digests.) Three specialty services also cover case law specifically dealing with the federal rules: *Federal Rules Decisions*, *Federal Rules Service*, and *Federal Rules of Evidence Service.*

2. Other Resources

Many excellent treatises cover federal rules. Some of the best known are *Moore's Federal Practice* (3d ed., LexisNexis 1997), Wright and Miller's *Federal Practice and Procedure* (Thomson Reuters 1978), and *Weinstein's Federal Evidence* (2d ed., LexisNexis 1997). These and many others provide extraordinary detail in their discussion of the various federal rules and are updated on a regular basis.

Chapter 9

Updating with Citators

I. What Is a Citator?

The case law of the United States uses as its basis the concept of precedent. That is, once a decision is made in a case, the decision not only applies to the parties in that particular case, but also serves as an example to future judges on how to decide cases that involve the same legal issue. Newer cases dealing with the same issue of law will often refer back to an older case.

A citator provides a list of all of the times a case is referred to—positively or negatively—in newer cases.[1] Until the 1990s, the major citator in the United States was known as *Shepard's Citations*. Print volumes of *Shepard's Citations* existed for every major case reporter. After the entry for each case, *Shepard's Citations* provided a list of all of the newer cases that referred back to that particular case. *Shepard's Citations* also provided an analysis of how the newer cases viewed the decision the court made in the older case.

During the 1990s, electronic citators began to replace the print editions. Shepard's Citations, Inc. was purchased by LexisNexis and started being featured exclusively on Lexis' online service. Left without a citator service, Thomson Reuters (known at that time as West Publishing) launched a competing service called KeyCite as part of its Westlaw service. As of 2011, relative newcomer Bloomberg Law also offers a citator service, called BCite, as part of its online legal database. Electronic services both reduced the number of steps required to locate all of the cases that used a particular older case for legal authority and provided greater detail about how the newer cases viewed the decision in the older case. Most law firms and many law libraries have eliminated their print versions of *Shepard's Citations* in favor of one of the online versions.

---

1. While this introduction speaks only of cases, many authorities can be updated using citators. Statutes, administrative regulations, and secondary sources are all the subject of citator lists. Further, the list of sources referring to the case, statute, regulation, or other source includes not just cases but other authorities as well.

II. Why Use a Citator?

A. Ensure Cases Are Still Good Law

One reason to use a citator is to determine if a particular case is still good law. Once a case is published in a reporter, it remains available to the public regardless of any future changes in the law. For example, *Plessy v. Ferguson* (the case that created the "separate but equal" doctrine) is still easily locatable in the *United States Reports*. There is no indication in the text of this case or anywhere else in the reporter volume that it has not been the law of the United States for more than 60 years. While some cases like *Plessy v. Ferguson* are overruled, many others have law that was altered, but not overruled, by later opinions. Newer cases could agree with older decisions, they could expand the older decision to cover new fact patterns, they could limit the situations to which the older decision applied, or they could overturn only a portion of the older decision. Failing to find the most current law or using a case that has been overturned can result in public embarrassment for your law office, sanctions from a judge, or even malpractice lawsuits.

B. Find Other Cases on the Same Legal Issue

Looking up a case in a citator will often lead to other cases on the same legal issue. As noted in the introduction to this chapter, the system of case law in the United States relies on the concept of precedent. In order to prove that precedent is being followed, judges in newer cases cite older cases as authority when writing the opinion. A citator identifies all newer cases that use a particular opinion as authority. There is a good chance, since the older case is being cited as authority, that both cases are on the same legal topic. Typically, cases from the same jurisdiction are listed first, then cases from other jurisdictions follow.

C. Find Secondary Sources on the Same Legal Topic

Citators also provide references to secondary sources that have cited a particular case. Both KeyCite and Shepard's provide references to law journals, treatises, and court documents. Locating secondary sources that cite a case can be trickier than it appears. Since KeyCite is part of Westlaw, which is owned by Thomson Reuters, treatises published by Thomson Reuters will appear in the KeyCite list, but treatises owned by LexisNexis will not appear. Shepard's lists treatises which are owned by LexisNexis (including books published under the Matthew Bender imprint), but not treatises published by

Thomson Reuters. Occasionally, a treatise published by publishers other than LexisNexis or Thomson Reuters (such as Wolters Kluwer or Bloomberg BNA) will appear in the lists, but even this is unusual. KeyCite also provides a list of locations in *American Law Reports* where the case has been cited, but Shepard's does not. Bloomberg Law provides citations to secondary sources from its Bloomberg BNA division and occasionally to secondary sources by other publishers, but usually not to law journals or materials printed by Thomson Reuters or LexisNexis.

III. How to Use Online Citators

A. KeyCite on Westlaw

KeyCite is available for all cases and statutes that are available on Westlaw. Its coverage is less complete for regulations, administrative decisions, and secondary sources, but some coverage for these materials does exist.

1. Accessing KeyCite

KeyCite can be accessed in two different ways. First, by typing "kc:" followed by a citation into the main search box that appears at the top of the main Westlaw screen (example: **kc: 514 US 1**), or second, by clicking on the "Negative Treatment," "History," or "Citing References" tabs at the top of any document displayed on Westlaw. (See Figure 9-1 for a sample Westlaw document page showing the tabs.) If the document does not have these tabs, or the tabs are greyed out, KeyCite is not available for that document. Occasionally, only the "Negative Treatment" tab or the "History" tab (or both) is greyed out. This means that, while KeyCite information is available for that document, there is no negative treatment or no history (or both—if both tabs are greyed out) for that document. Clicking on the red, yellow, or blue and white striped flag at the top of any document (if there is a flag displayed), will automatically display the "Negative Treatment" tab. Typing kc: followed by the citation into the main search bar will display the "Negative Treatment" tab if there has been any negative treatment. If there has not been any negative treatment, KeyCite will show the "Citing References" tab instead.

2. Navigating the KeyCite Tabs

After accessing the KeyCite screen for a document, it is easy to access the different features of KeyCite using the tabs at the top of the document. There are usually six tabs at the top of each document (see Figure 9-1). The "Docu-

Figure 9-1. Case from Westlaw Showing KeyCite Tabs

Image reprinted with permission from Thomson Reuters.

ment" tab will always display the text of the original document. The "Filings" tab displays any court documents that were filed in that particular case. Not all court documents are accessible through Westlaw, but Westlaw tries to provide access to the major briefs in each case. (For information on how to find additional court documents, see Chapter 11.)

The next three tabs are the ones that actually show KeyCite information. The "Negative Treatment" tab lists all of the newer cases that have commented negatively on the document being shown. For checking to see if a case is still valid, the "Negative Treatment" screen is the most important. It is this history that shows how courts have treated the decision reached in this case. The "Negative Treatment" screen is divided into two sections. The first section "Negative Direct History" shows any negative history in the litigation process involving this case. This list can show whether the case was reversed or altered on appeal. A black box with the word "KeyCited" in white text following the name of the case indicates which case is being checked. The screen also indicates the most negative case with a red box with "Most Negative" in white lettering following the name of the most negative case. There are two types of negative history. First, a case can have negative direct history. This means that the case being

Figure 9-2. KeyCite Negative Direct History

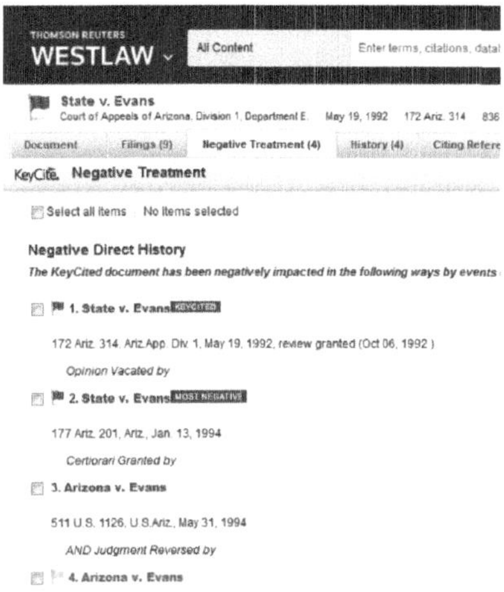

Image reprinted with permission from Thomson Reuters.

KeyCited was overturned on appeal. The case shown in Figure 9-1 does not have any negative direct history (although it does have 42 negative citing references). For an example of a negative direct history screen, see Figure 9-2.

Following the direct history, KeyCite lists "Negative Citing References." These are sources that KeyCite has identified as providing important negative treatment of the case, such as cases that may have overruled your case or questioned the decision reached in your case. See Figure 9-3 for a sample "Negative Citing References" screen. If you have limited time to update a case, you should at least skim the sources in this section. The "Negative Citing References" section looks a little different from the "Negative Direct History" section and contains additional information. Negative citing references are listed in a table (Note: the table is not sortable by column as of the time of this writing). The first column contains a check box that allows selecting just certain cases to print or compare. The second column of the table shows the specific way the newer case treated the document being KeyCited. The third column shows the name and citation of the newer case as well as some detail about the citing case. Clicking on the name of a citing reference will display the newer case. To locate where the older case is discussed in the newer case, click the forward green arrow next to the words "Search Term" that appear just under the tabs.

Figure 9-3. KeyCite Negative Citing References

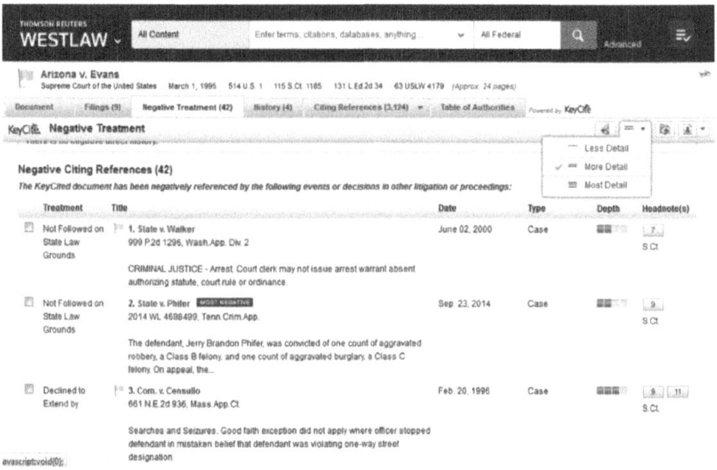

Image reprinted with permission from Thomson Reuters.

The amount of detail can be changed by using the pull-down menu on the left hand of the screen (shown in pulled-down mode in Figure 9-3). Some other symbols can also appear in column three. The most negative document is identified with a red box with white lettering. Certain cases may also have a right-handed quote symbol following the name of the case. This symbol means that the newer case quotes directly from the case being cited. The fourth column indicates the date of the newer case. Column five shows the type of document (for negative citing references the document type will most always be "case"). Column six indicates the depth of treatment the newer cases gives the older, cited case. There are four levels of treatment (from most to least amount of treatment): Examined, Discussed, Cited, and Mentioned. Finally, the last column shows which headnote numbers of the older case are discussed in the newer case. Placing your cursor over the headnote number will generate a pop-up window showing the topic, key number, and text of the headnote.

The "History" tab gives a graphical representation of the history of the case. This tab is divided into two frames. The left-hand frame lists the direct history

Figure 9-4. Sorting Options Menu for Citing References Table

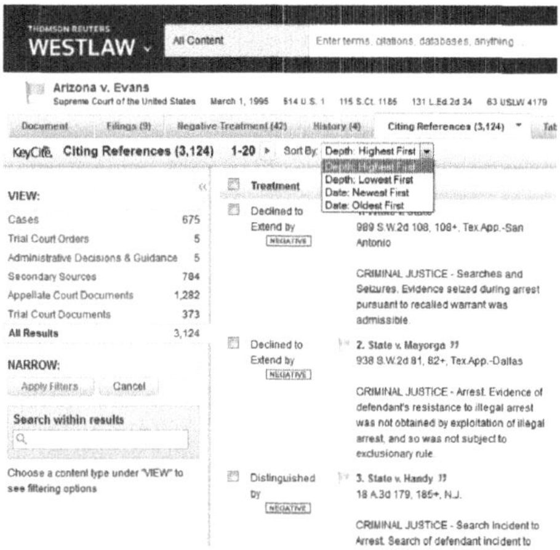

Image reprinted with permission from Thomson Reuters.

of the document while the right-hand frame gives a graphical representation of the history of the case.

To obtain the most comprehensive list of citing sources, choose the "Citing References" tab. The "Citing References" page lists all cases and other sources that have referenced this particular document. The "Citing References" page combines visual characteristics of both the "History" page and the "Negative Treatment" page, but works differently than either one of the other pages. See Figure 9-4 for a sample "Citing References" page. Like the "History" page there are two frames. The frame on the left side of the screen has two sections: "View" and "Narrow." Under the "View" heading, researchers can choose which type of document they would like to see. The types of documents that have used the case being cited as authority are listed and the number of each type of document is shown. The "Narrow" section allows researchers to limit the number of results. When the "Citing References" page first appears, the "Apply Filters" box under the "Narrow" section is greyed out. Once a document type is selected, the button becomes active. In addition to making the "Apply Filters" button active, selecting a type of document also causes the types of filters available for that document type to appear in the left frame. These filters are discussed below.

The right frame contains the same table discussed in the "Negative Citing References" paragraph, above. There are two main differences between the table on the "Citing References" page and the table on the "Negative Citing References" page. On the "Citing References" page, the table can be sorted by either depth of treatment or by date. This can be done by using the pull-down menu that appears directly below the tabs (shown expanded in Figure 9-4) or by clicking on the word "Date" or the word "Depth" in the header row of the table. The other difference is in the types of documents shown in the fifth column of the table. On the "Negative Citing References" page the only type of document shown was "Case." In the citing references table, there are literally dozens of types of documents identified.

The final tab is the "Table of Authorities" tab. The "Table of Authorities" is almost the exact opposite of the KeyCite tabs. Instead of showing how newer cases treated the case being cited, the "Table of Authorities" tab shows all of the cases that the case being KeyCited relied on for authority. The table on this page can be sorted by the name of the cases, the depth of treatment, and whether the current document quoted from the older case or not. In addition, the last column of the table shows the exact page where the older case was referenced in the current case.

3. Analyzing KeyCite Flags

KeyCite has assigned a flag to each document that has been modified to the point where its value is now considered questionable. This flag serves as a quick guide to the current legal status of the document (i.e., whether the case, statute, or regulation is still good law). When viewing a document, the flag, if there is one, can be found at the top left corner of the case viewing page—above the tabs, next to the case name. The flag also appears just above the beginning of the case, along with an explanation of why Westlaw is attaching that flag to the case (or other document).

Westlaw currently uses three flags to indicate negative case history. A red flag means that the case is no longer good law for at least one point of law in its home jurisdiction. A red flag does not necessarily mean that the case is no longer good law for the point of law you are researching, so it is important to read the case identified in the explanation next to the KeyCite flag to determine which points of law were affected. A yellow flag indicates that a document has some negative treatment, but no points of law in the case have specifically been overturned. Finally, a blue and white striped flag indicates that a case has been appealed to the U.S. Courts of Appeal or the U.S. Supreme Court.

4. Limiting the Search Results

If your case has been cited by many other sources, you may want to limit the KeyCite search results to those sources with particular relevance to your research project. For example, the case shown in Figure 9-4 has 3,124 documents which cite to it. Sources with particular relevance may be sources from a specific jurisdiction, sources that deal with the headnote (or headnotes) in which you are most interested, or specific types of documents such as cases, court documents, or secondary sources.

To limit a KeyCite display, first select the "Citing References" tab as it is the only tab that will allow filters. Next, choose the type of document. When most document types are chosen, they may show subcategories that allow limiting the search further. For example, for the case shown in Figure 9-4, clicking the "Secondary Sources" category allows the user to further limit the search to ALR only, law reviews only, or other (presumably treatises and CLE materials). The only document type that does not show subcategories is the "Cases" document type.

Once the type (and subtype) of document is selected, then additional filters can be applied. Different types of documents have different filters available and the filters can be combined for extremely effective searches. All document types allow you to search within results. You can use "Search within results" as a way of customizing their limitations. "Search within results" tells KeyCite to limit the display to documents that contain the word(s) or phrase(s) specified in the search box. Most document types also allow you to limit the display by date, depth of treatment, and headnotes from the KeyCited case that were discussed in the newer document. To search for a headnote topic, select the check box next to the topic. To select a specific headnote, use the "Specify" button next to the headnote topic. The button pulls up a pop-up window that allows users to select specific headnotes. For cases, researchers can also view only negative results, hide negative results, view only reported cases, view only unreported cases, or limit the display to cases from specific jurisdiction(s).

5. Understanding Symbols Next to Citing Cases

Researchers are often confused by the symbols preceding the names of the cases that are shown in the "Negative Treatment" or "Citing References" tables. KeyCite places symbols in front of those cases to provide an easy way of providing information on the status of the newer case. This symbol indicates only the status of the newer case and does not indicate any impact on the case actually being KeyCited.

6. Reading and Analyzing the Cases That Cite Your Case

While the flag is useful as a quick guide to the status of the document, it is only a preliminary indicator and represents the Westlaw editor's interpretation of the status of a particular case, statute, or regulation. Although the editor's interpretations are often correct, they sometimes differ from the actual language of the court. Relying on the flag is not a substitute for actually reading the case(s) that KeyCite indicates have affected the case which you are KeyCiting.

Just because a KeyCite symbol provides a quick indication that a case may or may not be good law does not mean that there is no need to read the newer cases. A KeyCite symbol which indicates that there is negative history (by using a red flag) does not necessarily mean that the case is no longer good law. It only means that there is a possibility that it may not be good law. You must read the newer case to determine its effect on the older case. Similarly, just because a case (or other document) does not have a red flag does not mean that the law discussed in it has not been materially changed by a newer case. There is no substitute for reading the newer cases for yourself and determining, for yourself, what effect the newer case has on the law discussed in the older case.

B. Shepard's on Lexis Advance

The sources that can be Shepardized on Lexis Advance are not identical to those covered by KeyCite, but for most researchers the differences are not noticeable.

1. Accessing Shepard's

Access to Shepard's on Lexis Advance can be obtained by following one of three different paths. The first two paths are from within the text of documents. First, each document has a "Shepardize® this document" link in a box to the right of the text of the document. Second, each document that can be Shepardized also has a Shepard's symbol to the left of the document name. (See Table 9-1, below, for a list of symbols.) These two methods of accessing Shepard's send you directly to the Shepard's entry for the case (or other document) you were viewing. Third, Shepard's can be accessed from the main Lexis Advance screen by typing "Shep:" followed by a citation. For example: **Shep: 514 U.S. 1.**

2. Navigating the Types of Shepard's Lists

After clicking on the "Shepardize" link or the Shepard's symbol or entering Shep: followed by a citation into the main search bar, the Shepard's listing for

Figure 9-5. Shepard's Citing Decisions Screen

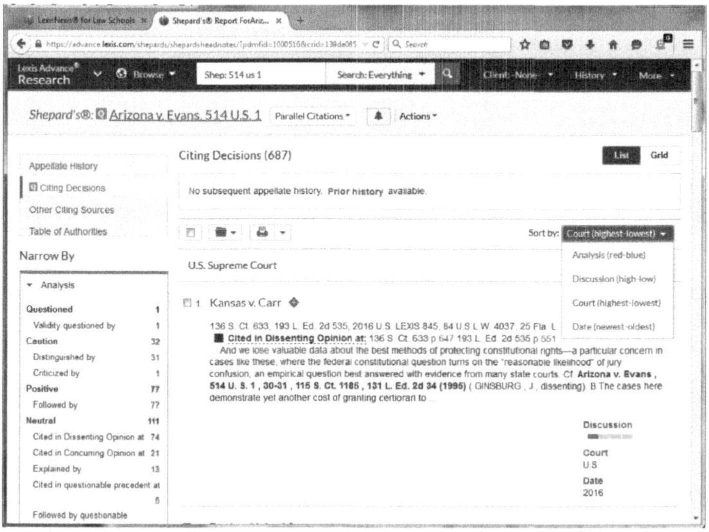

Image reprinted with permission from LexisNexis. Copyright 2017. LexisNexis, a division of Reed Elsevier, Inc. All rights reserved. LexisNexis and the Knowledge Burst logo are registered trademarks of Reed Elsevier, Inc.

that case will appear. The screen is divided into two frames. The left frame displays the type of Shepard's screens which are available for that document. The right frame shows a list of citations for the case being Shepardized. The default screen is "Appellate History" showing how the case being Shepardized worked its way through the court system. The document being Shepardized is indicated by the phrase "Citation you Shepardized" in red text. This case history can be shown in either list form or in map form, which is a graphical map showing how the case proceeded through the court system, similar to the history tab in KeyCite.

The "Citing Decisions" screen lists all of the documents that have used the document being Shepardized as authority. The list can be sorted by date (newest first), court (highest first), analysis (most negative first), or discussion (highest discussion first). See Figure 9-5. The entry for each citing decision provides some very specific information. The top of the entry gives the name and citation of the citing decision, a link to the exact page(s) where the original case was cited, an explanation of the treatment by the newer case, and a short snippet of text from the citing opinion showing the citation. Choosing the "Citing Decisions" screen also activates the list of filters in the left frame. These filters are discussed below.

In addition, each entry shows the level of discussion the newer case gives the case being Shepardized. Shepard's has four levels of treatment (from most to least): Analyzed, Discussed, Mentioned, and Cited. Each entry also shows the court that decided the newer case and the date of the newer case. Some entries show which headnote numbers from the older case are discussed in the newer case. Keep in mind that these are LexisNexis headnote numbers, not Thomson Reuters headnote numbers so if you have a copy of a case from Westlaw or from a print West reporter, the headnote numbers will not match. Placing the cursor over the headnote number will show the headnote topic.

The "Other Citing Sources" screen shows documents, other than cases that have used the document being Shepardized as authority. This screen can include many types of secondary sources, as well as statutes, regulations, and administrative materials. Filters are also available for these types of materials, but there are fewer filters than for cases.

Finally, the "Table of Authorities" screen. Much like the "Table of Authorities" screen in KeyCite, the "Table of Authorities" screen shows all of the cases that the case being Shepardized relied on for authority. The screen can be sorted by the court that decided the older opinion (highest to lowest court) or the analysis (most negative to least negative). Each entry shows the name and citation of the case used as authority, the page on which the older case was cited, the court that decided the older opinion, the date of the older opinion, and the level of discussion the case being Shepardized gives the older opinion.

3. Analyzing the Shepard's Symbols

While KeyCite only assigns flags to cases with negative treatment, Shepard's assigns a symbol to each document that is capable of being updated. This symbol serves as a quick guide to the current legal status of the document (i.e., whether the case, statute, or regulation is still good law). When you are viewing a document, the symbol appears to the left of the case name. The symbol is useful as a quick guide to the status of the document, but it is only a preliminary indicator of the Shepard's editor's interpretation of the status of a particular case, statute, or regulation. The editor's interpretations are often correct; however, relying on the symbol shown is not a substitute for actually reading the cases that Shepard's indicates have affected the case on which you are relying. Clicking on the case (or secondary source) name of a citing reference in Shepard's will take you to the exact page on which the case being Shepardized is

Table 9-1. Shepard's Treatment Symbols

Shepard's Symbol	Meaning
Red stop sign	Negative treatment, one or more points of law in the case may no longer be good law in one or more jurisdictions.
Orange square with letter "Q" in white	Negative treatment. The validity of one or more points of law has been brought into question in one or more jurisdictions, but no points of law have been specifically invalidated.
Yellow triangle	Possible negative treatment, but has not been reversed or overruled.
Green diamond	Citations to the document exist and are not negative. Generally indicates positive treatment.
Blue circle with white "A" or "I"	Citations to the document exist. Usually indicates string citations.

cited in the newer case. This provides a quick way to determine what the newer case actually says about the case you were Shepardizing. Table 9-1 shows a list of symbols found on Shepard's.

4. Limiting Shepard's Results

If your case has been cited by many other sources, you may want to limit the Shepard's search results to those sources with particular relevance to your research project. Sources with particular relevance may be sources from a specific jurisdiction, sources dealing with the headnote (or headnotes) in which you are most interested, or specific types of sources such as cases. There are several ways in which to limit a Shepard's display, all of which can be located in the left frame on the "Citing Decisions," "Other Citing Sources," or "Table of Authorities" pages.

Citing decisions and the Table of Authorities can be limited in several ways using the filters in the left frame. First, they can be limited by the analysis given, so that a researcher can see just the cases that questioned the case being Shepardized, or just the cases that followed the case being Shepardized. The Shepard's display can also be limited by court(s), by level of discussion, by the headnote discussed, by date, or by keywords entered by the user in the "Search Within Results" box. These filters can be combined for even more effective searching.

Citations on the "Other Citing Sources" page can be limited by type of document, date, or custom keywords using the "Search Within Results" box, or any combination of these filters.

5. Understanding Symbols Next to Citing Cases

Do not be confused by the symbols following the names of the cases on the "Appellate History" or "Citing Decisions" screens. These symbols provide easy information on the status of the newer case, but do not indicate any impact on the case you are Shepardizing.

6. Reading and Analyzing the Cases That Cite Your Case

As with KeyCite flags, a Shepard's symbol simply provides a quick indication that a case may or may not be good law. The symbol does not mean that reading the newer cases is not necessary. A Shepard's symbol indicating negative history (a red stop sign) means there is a possibility that at least one legal point in the case may not be good law in at least one jurisdiction, but it does not necessarily indicate which legal point has been overruled or which jurisdictions no longer follow that rule. Similarly, the lack of a red stop sign does not mean that the law discussed in a case has not been materially changed by a newer case. Reading the newer case and determining what effect it has on the law discussed in the older case is essential.

C. BCite on Bloomberg Law

1. Accessing BCite

Access to BCite on Bloomberg Law can be obtained only by first accessing a case for which BCite is available. Citation information from BCite can be obtained by clicking on the "Direct History," "Case Analysis," or "Citing Documents" tabs at the top of any court opinion shown on Bloomberg Law. Full BCite information is available only for case law. Other types of documents have limited or no BCite information. If the document does not have these tabs, or the tabs are greyed out, BCite is not available for that document.

2. Navigating the BCite Tabs

Accessing the different features of BCite is easy using the tabs at the top of the document. For court opinions, there are usually five tabs at the top of each document. The "Document" tab will always display the text of the original document.

Tabs two, three, and five are the ones that actually show BCite information. The "Direct History" page shows how the case being BCited moved through the court system. It has two frames. The left frame allows users to filter the results, while the right frame shows the direct history of the case. The opinion being BCited is highlighted in blue.

The "Case Analysis" screen has two frames. The left frame shows a list of filters that can be used to narrow the number of cases shown. These filters are discussed below. The right frame lists all of the documents that have used the document being BCited as authority. The list can be sorted by date (newest first), court (highest first), citing case analysis (negative first), or citation frequency (highest discussion first). The entry for each citing decision first gives the analysis of the treatment by the newer case (i.e., whether the newer case followed the older case, overruled the older case, etc.), then the list gives a symbol showing the status of the newer case. Next, the name and citation of the citing decision is shown. Clicking on the name of a citing reference will display the newer case. Finally, a bar showing the citation frequency is shown with the number of blue squares in the bar representing how many times the newer case cited the document being BCited. Just below this information is a pull-down arrow and the word "Extracts." Clicking on the arrow displays an extract from the newer case showing how and where the older case was used as authority. Extracts can be opened for all cases via a pull-down menu in the upper right corner of the screen (just below the tabs).

To obtain the most comprehensive list of citing sources, choose the "Citing Documents" tab. The "Citing Documents" tab lists all cases and other sources that have referenced this particular case. Federal statutes do not have this tab available. The "Citing Documents" page looks somewhat similar to the "Case Analysis" page. Like the other pages there are two frames. Just like the other pages, the frame on the left side of the screen shows filters that can be used to limit the number of documents displayed. The frame on the left side of the screen has two sections: "Content Type" and "Date." Under the "Content Type" heading, researchers can choose which type of document they would like to see. The types of documents which have used the case being cited as authority are listed and the number of each type of document is shown. Selecting a type of document also causes the types of filters available for that document type to appear in the left frame. These filters are discussed below. The "Date" section allows researchers to limit the documents shown to a specific date range. Once a document type is selected, the button becomes active. The right frame shows a list of all documents that have cited the case as authority. Choosing a type of document also brings up the sorting features for that document type.

The final tab is the "Table of Authorities" tab. The "Table of Authorities" is almost the exact opposite of the other BCite tabs. Instead of showing how newer cases treated the case being cited, the "Table of Authorities" tab shows all of the cases that the case being BCited relied on for authority. This screen looks almost identical to the "Case Analysis" screen.

Table 9-2. BCite Treatment Symbols

BCite Symbol	Meaning
Red box with white negative sign	Negative treatment, one or more points of law in the case may no longer be good law in one or more jurisdictions.
Orange square with circle	Case has been superseded by a statute.
Yellow square with white triangle	Negative treatment. The validity of one or more points of law has been brought into question in one or more jurisdictions, but no points of law have been specifically invalidated.
Blue square with slash mark	One or more courts have differentiated this opinion based on differences in the facts or law.
Green square with plus sign	Citations to the document exist and are not negative, generally indicating positive treatment.
Grey square with plus sign	No courts have cited to this opinion.

3. Analyzing the BCite Symbols

BCite assigns a symbol to each case. This symbol serves as a quick guide to the current legal status of the document (i.e., whether the case is still good law). When viewing a document, the symbol can be found to the left of the case name. While the symbol is useful as a quick guide to the status of the document, it is only a preliminary indicator and represents the BCite editor's interpretation of the status of a particular case. Although the editor's interpretations are often correct, they sometimes differ from the actual intent of the court. Relying on the symbol shown is not a substitute for actually reading the cases that BCite indicates have affected the case on which you are relying. Clicking on the case (or secondary source) name of a citing reference in BCite will take you to the newer case. Table 9-2 shows a list of symbols used on BCite.

4. Limiting BCite Results

If your case has been cited by many other sources, you may want to limit the BCite search results to those sources with particular relevance to your research project. Sources with particular relevance may be sources from a specific jurisdiction or specific types of sources such as cases. There are several ways in which to limit a BCite display, all of which can be located in the left frame on the "Case Analysis," "Citing Documents," or "Table of Authorities" pages.

Cases on the "Case Analysis" and the "Table of Authorities" screens can be limited in several ways using the filters in the left frame. The BCite display can be limited by treatment of the citing cases, court(s), citation frequency, court, date, or judge who decided the opinion. These filters can be combined for even more effective searching. Choosing the "Citing Decisions," then choosing "Court Opinions" activates different ways of limiting the case display.

Citations on the "Citing Documents" page must be limited by type of document before other filters (other than date) become available. "Books & treatises," "Law Reports," and law journals can then be limited by publisher or title. Court Opinions can be limited by jurisdiction, court, topic, or judge. Interestingly, most of these options are not available for case law on the "Case Analysis" page. Court orders can be limited by court. Administrative documents can be limited by jurisdiction and agency. Dockets and pleadings can be limited by the nature (i.e., topic) of the suit, the jurisdiction, and the court.

5. Understanding Symbols Next to Citing Cases

BCite places symbols in front of the titles of citing cases to indicate the status of the newer case or the status of the older case on the "Table of Authorities" screen. This symbol does not indicate any impact on the case actually being BCited.

6. Reading and Analyzing the Cases That Cite Your Case

A BCite symbol simply provides a quick indication that a case may or may not be good law. The symbol does not mean that reading the newer cases is not necessary. A BCite symbol indicating negative history (a red box with a white negative sign) means there is a possibility that at least one legal point in the case may not be good law in at least one jurisdiction, but it does not necessarily indicate which legal point has been overruled or which jurisdictions no longer follow that rule. Similarly, the lack of a red box does not mean that the law discussed in a case has not been materially changed by a newer case. Reading the newer case and determining what effect it has on the law discussed in the older case is essential.

D. Alerts

KeyCite, Shepard's, and BCite all offer the ability to "keep an eye on" the status of a particular case. This could be useful for monitoring the status of key cases that are frequently used in briefs or other documents submitted by a particular firm. For example, a firm that regularly submits briefs for clients on either side of the abortion debate would want to keep an eye on *Roe v. Wade*, both for status changes and to instantly know about newer cases that have cited *Roe.* Persons wanting to "keep an eye on" the status of a case can use a KeyCite Alert on KeyCite, a Shepard's Alert on Shepard's, or a citation alert on BCite. KeyCite and Shepard's use a button with a bell icon to set up their alert. On Westlaw, this bell icon appears on the right side of the document page, just under the tabs. On Lexis Advance, the bell icon appears on any Shepard's page at the top of the screen. BCite has a "Create Citation Alert" link at the bottom of the left-hand frame of the "Citing Documents" page.

Alerts on all three services work very similarly. An alert can be set to appear upon logging into the parent service or can be set to e-mail the user at either specified intervals or whenever a new document uses the case being monitored as authority. Alerts can also be set to only record certain types of documents that cite the monitored case (such as only cases or only law reviews) or only report if newer documents treat the case being monitored in a certain way (i.e., only negative cases).

Chapter 10

Secondary Sources and Practice Aids

In many situations, the best starting point for a legal research project is a secondary source. A secondary source is a work that describes and explains a particular area of law. Secondary sources are often contrasted with primary sources, which are created by courts, legislatures, and regulatory agencies. Common secondary sources are legal encyclopedias, treatises, practice guides, law reviews, and bar journals. By consulting a secondary source early, a researcher can gain an understanding of the law that underlies his or her case, identify leading cases or controlling statutes, and develop an understanding of any unique terms that can be used as keywords for searching print indexes and online databases.

This chapter discusses common secondary sources: legal encyclopedias, the *American Law Reports* (*ALR*), treatises, continuing legal education (CLE) publications, form books, and legal periodicals, as well as sources popular with Kentucky practitioners like Thomson Reuters' *Kentucky Practice* series. While many of these resources are available in electronic formats, this chapter focuses on print for several reasons. First, a good understanding of a source's organization as a printed book or set of books can make online searching more effective. Second, many lawyers find that using secondary sources in print is more efficient and cost-effective than using online sources. Often these works can easily be pulled from a shelf and an answer found in less time that it takes to log on to an online legal service, drill down to the proper database, and form a query. Moreover, while some secondary sources are inexpensive add-ons to a firm's computer-assisted legal research contract, others are expensive and will drive up the cost of every account in the office.

I. Nature of Secondary Sources

New legal researchers planning to use secondary sources should become familiar with the formal nature of legal books. While an ordinary book may have a simple table of contents and index, law books have a number of internal tools to assist researchers. First, the table of contents of law books—sometimes called a "title-outline"—is more detailed than that found in most non-legal books. As the alternate title suggests, it usually serves as a comprehensive outline of the material contained in the book, often down to the paragraph level.

In addition, there are several helpful tools at the front of law books. Most law books have tables of cases to assist researchers seeking commentary on a specific case. Researchers should also look for a table of abbreviations because it may contain abbreviations and other short-forms that are specific to that book.

The text of legal books typically looks different from that in most books. Law books are tightly organized, and some have numbered headers even at the paragraph level. These headers are often numbered decimally with the section symbol (§).

The indexes of legal books are also more elaborate. Researchers should expect abbreviations and many cross-references to other parts of the index; it is often a good idea to check the first page of an index to look for special instructions on its use.

Finally, if the book is updated (as most are), it is important to consult either the first page of pocket parts or the "last updated page" in loose-leaf sets to determine the frequency of updates.

II. Legal Encyclopedias

Legal encyclopedias are very good places to start a research project. They have well-researched and clearly written articles on most legal topics; a researcher can use them to become acquainted with the legal issues and terminology involved in that topic. There is no Kentucky legal encyclopedia, but the state's lawyers can benefit from using one of the two national encyclopedias, *Corpus Juris Secundum* (*CJS*) or *American Jurisprudence, 2d* (*Am. Jur. 2d*).

Both legal encyclopedias are organized into topical articles that are alphabetically arranged throughout the volumes of the set. They can be searched either by going directly to the volume in which the topic you are interested is located and scanning the topic's detailed outline or by using the set's index. To use the "topic-outline" method, scan the spines of the books in the set, which are labeled with the names of the first and last entries included (e.g., "Torts-Trusts") to find the wanted entry. Figure 10-1 on the following page shows an entry from *CJS* on the tort of defamation. As another example, to read about holographic wills, you would look through the "W" volumes to

Figure 10-1. *CJS*, Libel and Slander § 2

LIBEL AND SLANDER; INJURIOUS FALSEHOOD

§ 2 Defamation distinguished from other torts

Research References

West's Key Number Digest, Libel and Slander k1

The torts of defamation and invasion of privacy are separate torts because different injuries are caused and different interests are protected and compensated.

Although the torts of defamation and invasion of privacy are closely allied, and the same considerations[1] and legal standards[2] apply to each, they are separate and distinct torts,[3] because different injuries are caused[4] and different interests are protected and compensated.[5] Likewise, defamation and commercial disparage—

[1]U.S.—Cibenko v. Worth Publishers, Inc., 510 F. Supp. 761 (D.N.J. 1981).
Md.—Phillips v. Washington Magazine, Inc., 58 Md. App. 30, 472 A.2d 98 (1984).

[2]Md.—Phillips v. Washington Magazine, Inc., 58 Md. App. 30, 472 A.2d 98 (1984).

[3]U.S.—Cibenko v. Worth Publishers, Inc., 510 F. Supp. 761 (N.J. 1981); Fogel v. Forbes, Inc., 500 F. Supp. 1081 (E.D. Pa. 1980).

[4]U.S.—Bolduc v. Bailey, 586 F. Supp. 896 (D. Colo. 1984).
Kan.—Dominguez v. Davidson, 266 Kan. 926, 974 P.2d 112 (1999).
W. Va.—Crump v. Beckley Newspapers, Inc., 173 W.Va. 699, 320 S.E.2d 70 (1983).

[5]Cal.—Selleck v. Globe International, Inc., 212 Cal. Rptr. 838 (2d Dist. 1985).

find the appropriate book, flip through the entries to find "Wills," and then scan the topic-outline for holographic or hand-written wills.

This method is very efficient if the researcher knows which entry covers the topic (and many veteran researchers do), but otherwise the index method is preferred. The annually issued indexes to both legal encyclopedias are very comprehensive and they cover several softbound volumes. These indexes are also somewhat complicated to use. Both use occasionally confusing short-hand abbreviations in boldface for the entries, so you should confirm the full title in the title of abbreviations at the beginning of the index. For example, in *CJS*, the article entry "Right to die" is abbreviated as "Die" in the index. In addition, cross-references to potentially better keywords are found throughout the index.

Table 10-1. *ALR 6th*, Contents of Volume 63

- Construction and Application of U.S. Const. Art. I, § 10, cl. 1, and State Constitutional Provisions Proscribing State Bills of Attainder.
- Workers' Compensation: Value of Expenses Reimbursed by Employer as Factor in Determining Basis for or Calculation of Amount of Compensation Under State Workers' Compensation Statute.
- Absolute Immunity for Failing to Disclose Exculpatory Evidence Under 42 U.S.C.A. § 1983 Following *Imbler v. Pachtman*, 424 U.S. 409, 96 S. Ct. 984, 47 L. Ed. 2d 128 (1976).
- Validity, Construction, and Application of State Trademark Counterfeiting Statutes.
- Validity of State Sex Offender Registration Laws Under Ex Post Facto Prohibitions.
- Validity, Construction, and Application of Placement Preferences of State and Federal Indian Child Welfare Acts.
- Liability for Injury on or in Connection with Escalator.

Thus, if you look up "Bookmaking" in the "B-C" volume of *Am. Jur. 2d* index, it refers you to "Gambling (this index)," which should be understood as a direction to find whatever volume of the index has the letter "G" on the spine. It is often useful to take notes so that every possibility is checked.

III. *American Law Reports*

While the *ALR* began its life as a law reporter, it currently serves primarily as a unique secondary source with national scope. When it started in 1919, it reprinted leading new cases from around the country with an article, called an "annotation," to explain the case and its context within American law. Now that the *ALR* is in its seventh series, the annotation/article is the main feature and the case is no longer appended.

ALR annotations discuss a narrow legal issue and describe how that issue is dealt with in jurisdictions around the nation (see Table 10-1). Each annotation collects leading cases and statutes from as many jurisdictions as have considered the legal issue in question, and often arranges this authority into legally significant categories. Every *ALR* annotation has a detailed topic-outline and internal index and has references to important treatises and practice guides.

ALR has seven series, and there are also three federal series that cover legal questions arising under the U.S. Constitution and federal legislation. There is a broad general index to the whole set and a shorter "quick index" that omits the largely out-of-date first and second series.

The *ALR* is an excellent source for finding persuasive authority because a typical annotation will outline the majority rule (i.e., the rule held by most states), listing every jurisdiction in support; the minority rule; and every gradation of judicial opinion in-between. You should check *ALR* early in your research because, while it only takes a few minutes to determine whether an on-point annotation exists, if one does, hours of research may be saved.

Annotations are updated with pocket parts and replacement annotations. Volumes since the third series have pocket parts to reflect new cases and minor changes in the law, but when the legal area covered by an annotation has undergone major changes, *ALR* editors issue a replacement annotation. The replacement version is published in the current series, as if it were a new annotation, and the pocket part entry for the old version will clearly indicate the replacement. For this reason, you must always check the pocket part. Almost all annotations in the first two series have been replaced, and most lawyers consider the set to begin with the first volume of *ALR 3d*.

IV. Treatises and Practice Guides

A. General Information

Treatises and practice guides are extremely valuable in legal research because they provide a comprehensive discussion of a discrete area of law that identifies and analyzes all leading cases, statutes, and regulations. The difference between treatises and practice guides is often a matter of degree but, in general, treatises concentrate on substantive legal analysis while practice guides seek to apply that law to drafting legal documents and trial practice. A typical treatise will break down a legal issue into all its constituent parts, and will describe and comment on all the relevant primary legal sources. Its content is mostly textual commentary, but it may have excerpts of primary documents and other useful matter in an appendix. Practice guides are more aimed at assisting lawyers in doing their work—drafting contracts and pleadings, managing discovery, and trying cases in courtrooms. Their pages are made up of concrete materials like checklists, sample pleadings, and even model opening statements, mock cross-examinations, and examples of jury instructions. As a practical matter, the line between the two types of secondary sources is often blurred, especially in those that focus on state law. Because of this, researchers should not neglect a legal treatise when looking for sample forms or be surprised that a state practice guide has commentary on substantive law.

Treatises can be found on a variety of topics and range in depth from the multi-volume Wright & Miller's *Federal Practice and Procedure*[1] to the more narrowly focused *Sutherland on Statutes and Statutory Construction*.[2] Some treatises are so authoritative that not citing them when expected may raise eyebrows. Robert Lawson's *Kentucky Evidence Law Handbook*, written by longtime University of Kentucky evidence professor and the chair of the committee that drafted the Kentucky evidence rules, is habitually cited in state courts.[3] Practice guides are focused more narrowly on the practical aspects of the law, but also cover a wide range of topics. There are book-length guides to allocating damages in wrongful death cases and multi-volume sets devoted to the drafting of federal securities law documents.

Like most law books, treatises and practice guides are typically updated, usually on an annual basis. The larger multi-volume sets are most often issued in loose-leaf binders and updated with replacement pages that the owner must file. Some smaller sets are updated with pocket parts, and certain one-volume titles are published each year in softbound format, usually with the issuing year added to the title. This last method makes the books more portable and creates a supply of "slightly used" copies around law offices. Treatises that are not as time sensitive are simply updated with new editions published when enough new material is collected.

You can find treatises and practice guides in most law libraries by using the physical or online library catalog. They are also regularly featured in the print and online catalogs of legal publishers like LexisNexis, Thomson Reuters, and Wolters Kluwer. Once an appropriate title is located, you can usually search it by index or by scanning the detailed title-outline that serves as the table of contents.

---

1. Charles A. Wright & Arthur R. Miller, *Federal Practice and Procedure* (4th ed., Thomson Reuters 2008). Please note that despite the 2008 publication date, this book and other books in the footnotes to this chapter have been updated with pocket parts, replacement volumes, or loose-leaf pages up to the present year.

2. Norman J. Singer and Shambie Singer, *Sutherland on Statutes and Statutory Construction* (7th ed., Thomson Reuters 2008). Prominent legal treatises often retain an author's name long after that author is no longer associated with the work. Jabez Gridley Sutherland, for example, has been dead since 1902.

3. Robert G. Lawson, *The Kentucky Evidence Law Handbook* (5th ed., LexisNexis 2013).

B. Kentucky Treatises and Practice Guides

Perhaps the most useful treatises and guides are those that examine the law of one state on a particular subject. Kentucky lawyers regularly advise young researchers that the best place to start research on a topic is to consult some long-recognized treatise or practice guide like Mapother on *Kentucky Collections* or Palmore's *Kentucky Jury Instructions.*[4]

One popular collection of state law treatises is the West division of Thomson Reuters' *Kentucky Practice* series. The set, which has absorbed some of the independent titles over the years, now has 23 volumes covering many, but not all, areas of Kentucky law (see Table 10-2). The *Kentucky Practice* titles mix detailed analysis of state law with practice materials, including sample forms. Each title has a title-outline and an individual index; an annually issued softbound index covers the whole set. Most volumes are hardbound books that are updated with pocket parts, but some are regularly replaced softbound books. The series is always evolving; many new titles have been added in recent years and the older ones have been renovated.

Thomson Reuters also maintains another line, the Kentucky Handbook Series, that has a somewhat greater practice orientation, but also combines legal analysis with practical assistance. Leading titles include Mapother and Canary on *Kentucky Collections* (which started its life with another publisher), Eades's *Kentucky Law of Damages*, and Osborne's *Trial Handbook for Lawyers*, all of which are issued as single-volume softbound books.[5] LexisNexis does not market any named series, but publishes titles like Lawson's influential evidence handbook and Nowka and Liebson's *Uniform Commercial Code of Kentucky.*[6]

Despite the coverage provided by these commercial titles, there are still many topics in Kentucky law without a treatise. These gaps in the literature are filled to a large extent by the many publications of the University of Kentucky's Office of Continuing Legal Education. The "UK CLE," as it is often called, publishes a number of publications in print and CD-ROM. Many of

---

4. William R. Mapother & Thomas L. Canary, Jr., *Kentucky Collections* (5th ed., Thomson Reuters 2016); John S. Palmore & William S. Cooper, *Kentucky Instructions to Juries* (5th ed., LexisNexis 2006).

5. William R. Mapother & Thomas L. Canary, Jr., *Kentucky Collections* (Thomson Reuters 2016); Ronald W. Eades, *Kentucky Law of Damages* (Thomson Reuters 2016); Thomas L. Osborne, *Trial Handbook for Lawyers* (Thomson Reuters 2016).

6. David J. Leibson & Richard H. Nowka, *The Uniform Commercial Code of Kentucky* (LexisNexis 2003).

Table 10-2. *Kentucky Practice* Series

Title	Volumes
Probate Practice and Procedure	1, 2
Real Estate Transactions	3, 3A
Methods of Practice	4, 4A, 5
Rules of Civil Procedure	6, 7
Criminal Practice and Procedure	8, 9
Substantive Criminal Law	10, 10A
Civil Procedure Forms	11, 12
Tort Law	13
Trial Practice	14
Domestic Relations	15, 16
Kentucky Corporation Law with Forms	17
Kentucky Workers' Compensation with Forms	18
Appellate Practice	19
Kentucky Motions in Limine	20
Kentucky Elements of an Action	21
Kentucky Summary Judgment and Related Termination Motions	22
Kentucky Elder Law	23
Index	Not numbered

its titles are the required reading for the year-round schedule of annual institutes and other CLE programs the agency organizes, but a publishing unit of the agency issues stand-alone treatises and handbooks. Some of the titles are widely used, especially the *Kentucky Legal Ethics Deskbook*, but the UK CLE also produces works like *Kentucky Administrative Law*, which cover areas of law untouched by commercial publishers. The materials from CLE programs, especially the UK CLE's nationally respected equine law institute, are important sources for new developments in Kentucky law.[7]

7. Todd B. Eberle et al., *Kentucky Legal Ethics Deskbook* (5th ed., Office of Continuing Legal Education, University of Kentucky College of Law 2016).

V. Legal Form Books

While some legal forms are included with treatise and practice guides, they are often collected into comprehensive sets. It is perhaps useful to note that a "legal form" should never be confused with a standardized form like an IRS 1040 that the user need only fill in the blanks. When lawyers use the term, they mean sample language and formatting examples, often liberally annotated with statutory and case law, which are used to assist attorneys in drafting documents. The "forms" in form books are samples of standard documents, sometimes only clauses, to be used as models for the formal documents that a lawyer will carefully tailor to the facts of a specific case. It is true that some legal transactions use standard forms, but those forms are typically found on government and court websites, not in law books.

There are three Kentucky form books regularly consulted by lawyers, all with slightly different focuses. *Baldwin's Kentucky Lawyer's Handbook with Forms* is aimed at lawyers practicing in state trial courts. It has practical guidance on drafting pleadings and motions in Kentucky district and circuit courts. It is divided into volumes on civil and criminal practice. It has the best coverage of criminal law and is a useful tool for both prosecutors and defense attorneys. *Caldwell's Kentucky Form Book* is more comprehensive in nature, and its forms are organized alphabetically by topic in four loose-leaf binders. Wyatt, Tarrant & Combs's *Kentucky Forms and Transactions* focuses narrowly on commercial law and estate planning.[8]

VI. Jury Instructions

Jury instructions are special types of forms. When juries retire to deliberate at the conclusion of a trial, they are guided by the written instructions of the judge, which clearly state the legal rules upon which they must decide the case. Often these instructions are drafted with the input of all the parties' lawyers and are their last chance to shape the verdict. (Jury instructions are also excellent guides to the essential elements in a cause of action that a lawyer must prove to sustain his or her case.) Unlike many states, Kentucky does not have officially adopted "pattern" jury instructions. However, Palmore and Cooper's *Kentucky*

---

8. *Baldwin's Kentucky Lawyer's Handbook with Forms* (Thomson Reuters 2015); Kevin P. Bucknam et al., *Caldwell's Kentucky Form Book* (5th ed., LexisNexis 2006); *Kentucky Forms and Transactions* (Thomson Reuters 1991).

Table 10-3. Kentucky Legal Periodicals

Major law reviews:
Kentucky Law Journal (University of Kentucky)
Northern Kentucky Law Review
University of Louisville Law Review
Bar journals:
Bench & Bar (Kentucky Bar Association)
Bar Briefs (Louisville Bar Association)
Lex Loci (Northern Kentucky Bar Association)
Bar News (Fayette County Bar Association)

Jury Instructions, which was developed by a former chief justice of the Kentucky Supreme Court, fills this role. The work, divided into volumes on civil and criminal law, has sample instructions derived from court documents.

VII. Legal Periodicals

When a new area of law arises, traditional secondary sources often find it difficult to incorporate these new issues into their detailed structure. Legal periodicals thrive on novelty and legal researchers get the best results by consulting law reviews, bar journals, and subject newsletters for information on new developments in the law. Table 10-3 lists some important Kentucky periodicals.

A. Law Reviews

Law reviews and journals contain articles on new questions in the law; the articles are written by law professors, judges, and practicing lawyers. Articles in law reviews analyze an issue in great depth, but they do not just describe the current law. A good law review article critiques that law in the light of new developments and then proposes new legal principles and theories of the law. Typically, law review articles cover topics of interest to the entire U.S. legal community. However, academic law reviews also publish student written "notes" or "comments," which are shorter pieces that often examine new issues in the jurisdiction where the school is located.

While there are some commercial legal journals, the majority of law reviews are sponsored by law schools and edited by student editorial boards made up of students chosen on the basis of good grades and proven writing ability. The articles are rigorously edited with an eye toward assuring that every assertion has a proper citation to an appropriate authority. Because of this, law review articles have a wealth of citations to statutes and case law. When an author says that a majority of states have adopted a particular legal rule, a researcher can expect a footnote with a statute or case from every state in the union that has weighed in on the issue.

Law reviews are published in soft-cover on a regular basis, usually four issues per volume year. Many but not all libraries bind the completed volumes and retain them permanently. Articles are not updated, so legal researchers often confine their searches to the most recent years. A small number of law reviews are shifting to an online only format.

B. Bar Journals

The articles in the periodicals of state and local bar associations do not usually have the depth and erudition of law reviews, but they offer greater currency and local scope. Another benefit is the close connection that their writers have to the courts and legislature in the jurisdiction. When a state adopts a new law, a lawyer involved with its passage will often write an article explaining the law and the thoughts of the legislature. Legal ethics articles are frequently written by members of the bar committee promulgating and adjudicating rules and, when the state court decides a major case, the issues are often debated in the columns of a local bar journal.

The greatest problem with bar journals is that they are less accessible (physically and intellectually) than law reviews. Many are not included in Westlaw and Lexis databases, and most are only indexed in print publications shelved at law libraries. However, the Kentucky Bar Association website has an online index covering the *Bench & Bar* and its predecessors from 1936 to present (https://www.kybar.org/page/bbindex).

C. Locating Articles

The method of finding law review and bar journal articles on a topic often depends on whether you are searching from an academic or county law library or from a law firm, because many useful resources are only affordable for academic institutions. This section will attempt to be sensitive to this issue.

The best method for identifying useful articles is to consult a legal periodical index, find appropriate articles, and then pull those articles from a database or from the stacks. Many law libraries subscribe to either one or both of the two print indexes, *Current Law Index* (CLI) or *Index to Legal Pe-*

riodicals (ILP), or one of their online counterparts, *LegalTrac* (based on the CLI) or *ILP Online.* Indexes, even online indexes, do not have the full text of articles, but they are designed to make finding articles relatively easy. Academic law libraries have traditionally maintained collections of legal periodicals in print that researchers can take to copiers to duplicate, but, increasingly, they also subscribe to HeinOnline, an online database of law reviews. HeinOnline articles can be downloaded or printed from library computers. (Because of the ease-of-use of HeinOnline, which has its own search engine, some law libraries have cancelled their online and print periodical indexes.)

Researchers confined to law firms, which do not usually purchase legal indexes or HeinOnline, often have access to full-text law review databases as part of the firm's Westlaw or Lexis package plans. Full-text searching of long and heavily footnoted law review articles requires precise formulation of searches. One commonly repeated tip suggests that researchers start by limiting their search to the titles of law reviews, which usually include a phrase summarizing the topic. In Westlaw, this requires the use of the "ti" prefix, for example, **ti("kentucky partnership law")**.

The recent explosion of legal blogs as well as the development of pre-press services like Social Science Research Network (SSRN) (http://www.ssrn.com) has provided researchers free access to law reviews posted on the Internet even before publication. Often law professors will post a recently written law review to SSRN before or simultaneously to submitting it to law reviews. Many authors post a link on their blog and invite comment from the blog's small circle of interested readers. After publication, authors usually, but not always, replace the pre-press article with the final version. Both services have rudimentary search engines, but the best tool to research these law reviews is Google Scholar (http://scholar.google.com), which indexes both services, as well as other public repositories of scholarly research. However, it is important to be careful when using these sources. Searches will often turn up articles that are so poorly reasoned and researched that they will never be published and are actually a menace to unwary researchers.

Chapter 11

Online Legal Research

I. Introduction

Online research is often necessary for conducting effective legal research. Unlike other types of online research, legal research requires a certain degree of knowledge and precision. It is important not only to know which resources are available, but also to have a working knowledge of the strategies involved in conducting good online legal research.

Following a brief review of whether to search in print or online, this chapter provides basic information about where to locate Kentucky legal information on the Internet (on both commercial services and free sites) and discusses some of the strategies that can be used to locate relevant statutes or cases on those websites.

II. Choosing between Print and Online

A good research strategy involves determining which format, electronic or print, will work best for the search being conducted. Some sources, such as unpublished opinions and some Kentucky administrative materials, exist only electronically, while other resources, such as certain treatises, exist only in print format. Excluding either format has the potential to cause you to miss important resources. If a particular source is available in both electronic and print formats, some researchers, especially newer legal professionals and students, believe that electronic is always better. Online resources have a number of advantages, but even fans of electronic research agree that print resources can often provide a better starting point. So which is better? While the answer is often "it depends," there are some good general rules when starting a legal research project.

Generally, certain tools work better in certain formats. Electronic research is usually the best starting point for cases (when looking for similar fact patterns or unpublished cases), law journals (from about 1990–present), Kentucky administrative materials (excluding the *Kentucky Administrative Regulations*), federal regulations, U.S. government documents, news resources, and citation services. Print research is usually more efficient for treatises, statutes, the *Kentucky Administrative Regulations*, cases (when looking for similar legal issues), and non-case documents produced prior to the mid-1990s. Which format is best for legislative history, legal encyclopedias, and *American Law Reports* annotations can vary depending on the age of the material and the type of search being conducted.

While a certain format may be more efficient for a certain legal resource tool, it does not mean that research would be impossible using another format. Good researchers not only know which format is more efficient, but also have developed a certain level of expertise with alternate formats so that, should the need arise, they can conduct research using any format.

III. Searching Online

The most effective method of using online services in conducting legal research involves five steps: 1) clarify the issue; 2) generate search terms; 3) choose the resource to be searched; 4) select a search technique; and 5) review and refine the search.

A. Clarify the Issue

First, carefully think through the legal issue. It is very easy to get sidetracked on materials that are close to the issue but not directly on point. For many researchers, it helps to write down the issue in a single sentence that summarizes the legal question to be researched. Writing down the issue can also help determine search terms that can be used, both for searching electronically and for searching indexes in print. Having a succinct written question can also help with the choice of which legal resources would provide the best starting points. If the question seems vague or the search terms are unclear, secondary sources may be the best starting point. If the question is clear and the search terms obvious, it may be better to go straight to statutes, regulations, or case law.

B. Generate Search Terms

Generate a comprehensive list of search terms, following the guidelines given in Chapter 1. Having a good list of search terms is extremely important

Table 11-1. Websites for Major Commercial Providers

Bloomberg Law	www.bloomberglaw.com
Casemaker (free to Ky. state bar members)	www.kybar.org (Use Casemaker link at top of screen)
Fastcase	www.fastcase.com
Lexis Advance	advance.lexis.com
VersusLaw	www.versuslaw.com
Westlaw	www.westlaw.com

for any type of legal research, but is essential in conducting online research because search engines are very literal. When looking for the word "car," a print index might refer the researcher to other terms such as "vehicle" or "automobile." A search engine will look only for the term "car" in the document. If the court or legislature used words such as "automobile," "motor vehicle," "truck," or "Ford," a search for the word "car" will not find that document. Thus, it is important not only to think of synonyms when generating search terms for an online search, but also to include broader terms, such as "motor vehicle," and narrower terms, such as "SUV" (or "sport utility vehicle"), in the search.

C. Choose the Resource to Search

1. Commercial Online Services vs. Free Websites

Electronic resources are generally divided into two areas: commercial services and free Internet sites. Commercial services tend to collect the largest amount of material and are the only websites that offer any editorial enhancements to the text of cases or statutes. By far, the largest commercial online services are Lexis Advance and Westlaw. These two services offer a full range of legal research products, including primary law (cases, statutes, and regulations), treatise materials, journals, and citator services. A third competing service, Bloomberg Law, started in 2010. With Bloomberg's purchase of legal publisher, the Bureau of National Affairs (BNA) in 2011, it became a more serious player in the online commercial legal services market. Other commercial services also exist, such as Casemaker, VersusLaw, or Fastcase. These smaller services typically do not provide as much material as Westlaw or Lexis. (See Table 11-1 for website addresses.) Usually, the smaller services do not offer treatises, law journals, or editorial enhancements such as headnotes or annotated statutes. Bloomberg Law offers access to BNA treatises, but does not add editorial content to cases or statutes and does not offer access to law journals. Bloomberg Law does have access to business materials, corporate financial documents and a vast collection of federal (and some state) docket materials not available on Westlaw or Lexis. While these smaller commercial services do not offer as much material, they can be much cheaper. Smaller law firms on limited budgets often use these services as the first line of electronic legal research.

Commercial services are not the only way to obtain legal materials online. The Internet is full of free websites that offer access to legal materials. Like anything else on the Internet, some sites are good and some sites are not so good. The key to using free websites is to first know which websites offer quality information. Much of the same information that can be obtained through commercial websites can also be obtained through free websites with a little effort. The downside to free websites is that they do not provide the same search capabilities as the commercial websites, frequently have access to only limited materials, and offer no editorial enhancements such as headnotes or annotations.

2. Kentucky Resources

a. Statutes and Regulations

While Kentucky statutes and regulations can easily be found on all of the commercial online services, Kentucky has some excellent free websites that provide online access to legal materials. The Legislative Research Commission, an arm of the Kentucky legislature, provides online access to a wide variety of legal materials on its website (http://www.lrc.ky.gov). Access to legal documents can be located under the heading "Kentucky Law" in the left frame of the Legislative Research Commission's main webpage. Under this section, you can find the most recent version of the Kentucky constitution, an unannotated version of the Kentucky Revised Statutes (http://www.lrc.ky.gov/Statutes/index.aspx), a current copy of the *Kentucky Administrative Regulations* (http://www.lrc.ky.gov/kar/frntpage.htm), and the *Kentucky Acts* (http://www.lrc.ky.gov/acts/mainacts.htm) dating back to 1995. Unlike the versions found on commercial services, this free version of the Kentucky Revised Statutes is not an official version,[1] although it is usually accurate. The usefulness of the statutes

1. To be an official version, a copy of the Kentucky Revised Statutes must meet the requirements of KRS 7.134. The electronic copy on the Legislative Research Commission's website does not meet all of the requirements and thus cannot be an official version.

portion of this website is limited because of the lack of annotations and the fact that it is not official, although it can still be quite useful if all that is needed is the text of the statute.

The administrative regulations section can also be quite useful. It is the most up-to-date version of Kentucky regulations, as it incorporates changes to the regulations each month. However, like the Kentucky Revised Statutes, the version of the *Kentucky Administrative Regulations* found on the Legislative Research Commission's website is also unofficial. In addition to providing access to the most up-to-date version of the *Kentucky Administrative Regulations*, the Legislative Research Commission's website also provides access to the most recent issue of the *Administrative Register of Kentucky*, the Agenda for the next meeting of the Administrative Regulation Review Subcommittee, and the cumulative index for the prior volume of the *Administrative Register* (the cumulative index for the most recent volume is included in the most recent issue).

Links to pending legislation can be found under the "Legislative Activity" section in the right (main) frame of the Legislative Research Commission's homepage. To access legislation which has passed during the current session choose the link for the "[current year] Regular Session *Legislative Record*" or the "[current year] Special Session *Legislative Record*" (if there was a special session). Past *Legislative Records* are available starting with the first 1997 special session. *Interim Legislative Records*, which contain the minutes of interim committee meetings, are available from 2008 to the present. These can be a valuable tool for tracing the legislative intent behind a particular statute. Also available is a link to video coverage of the House, Senate, and selected committees of both legislative bodies. This link directs users to the video archive maintained by Kentucky Educational Television (KET). KET's online video archive starts with the 2010 session, and can be directly accessed at http://www.ket.org/legislature/?archive. Like the *Interim Legislative Record*, the videos can be useful in determining legislative intent. Videos from older sessions can be obtained in physical format (i.e. DVD or VHS) from either the Legislative Research Commission or KET, but are not currently accessible online.

b. Court Materials

Once again, while judicial opinions can be found with ease on commercial online services, Kentucky case law can also be located on the Internet. While the Legislative Research Commission makes statutes, regulations, and other legislative materials available on its website, it does not provide access to court decisions. For court decisions, researchers have to rely on other websites. The most useful Kentucky-specific site is that of the Kentucky Court of Justice (http://courts.ky.gov). On this website, the Court of Justice provides access to judicial opinions from both the Kentucky Court of Appeals and the Kentucky Supreme Court. Both Supreme Court and Court of Appeals opinions are available via the same webpage (http://apps.courts.ky.gov/supreme/sc_opinions.shtm). Court of Appeals opinions are available from 1996 to the present, while Supreme Court opinions are available from 1999 to the present. The Court of Justice website includes both published and unpublished opinions. Each opinion is stored as a PDF file, and opinions are usually available on the website the same day they are released to the public. Unpublished opinions are also available through the commercial online services, but the coverage does not extend back as far. For example, Lexis Advance provides access to unpublished Kentucky opinions starting in 2003.

Access to other court materials is much more limited. Westlaw, Lexis Advance, and Bloomberg Law all provide some access to Kentucky briefs and pleadings. Westlaw's coverage begins in 1998 for trial court materials and 1999 for briefs. Lexis has trial court materials dating from as early as 1991 and briefs from as early as 1992. Bloomberg Law has the least amount of coverage for Kentucky with court filings from 2015 to the present for the Kentucky Supreme Court and from 2016 to the present for the Kentucky Court of Appeals.

Court briefs can also be located without access to a commercial online service. The Salmon P. Chase College of Law library provides access to court briefs starting in 1999 for the Kentucky Supreme Court and 2005 for the Kentucky Court of Appeals. Copies of the briefs (in PDF format) can be obtained from http://chaselaw.nku.edu/new/library/electronic_resources/ briefs_search.php.

c. Secondary Sources

For most Kentucky secondary sources, the only real electronic access is through the electronic databases on Westlaw and Lexis. Some newer journal articles can be located by searching sites such as SSRN (http://www.ssrn.com) or Google Scholar (scholar.google.com), but the results are really hit and miss. The only Kentucky secondary source which is readily available is the Kentucky bar journal, the *Bench & Bar*. Issues from the *Bench & Bar* are available via the bar association's website from January 2007 to the present (https://www.kybar.org//page/BB). Unlike the bar journals from most states, full indexes to the *Bench & Bar* are also available through the Bar association's website at https://www.kybar.org/page/bbindex.

3. *Federal Resources*

a. Statutes and Regulations

Finding federal statutes on the Internet is a relatively easy task. There is one problem with the version of the *United States Code* on the majority of free websites: the websites are so far out-of-date that the validity of the statutes is questionable. Most free websites provide access to the 2012 edition of the *United States Code*, as updated by the most recently printed official supplement. Unfortunately, the official supplement can be as many as three years behind. Some free websites are not even this up-to-date and have not updated their websites to reflect any changes since the 2012 edition of the *United States Code* was released.

There is one website that offers the most current version of the *United States Code* available in any format, as it does not wait on the release of the official supplement to update its version. This is the version of the *United States Code* located at the U.S. House of Representatives website (http://uscode.house.gov/). The Office of Law Revision Counsel of the House of Representatives is the entity that is tasked, under the federal statutes, with printing the *United States Code*.[2] Since they have the responsibility for maintaining the official database, they do not have to wait for the print edition to be published to update their version. The House's electronic version of the code is both completely up to date (with updates included each time a new public law is passed) and considered to be an official version. Each section of the Code from this website provides a statement of currency at the top of the page. Typically, this statement of currency shows the code is only one day out of date. Older editions and supplements of the *United States Code* (back to the 1994 edition) can also be searched using this website.

Like the *United States Code*, the free online version of the *Code of Federal Regulations* provided by the U.S. government is the most up-to-date version that can be obtained in any format. The Government Publishing Office (GPO) has three interrelated websites that provide access to the most current version of the *Code of Federal Regulations* and the *Federal Register*. GPO provides access to an official copy of the *Code of Federal Regulations* through its website (https://www.govinfo.gov/app/collection/CFR). The copy provided on this website is identical to the print version of the *Code of Federal Regulations*. Access to the *Federal Register* can also be obtained via the GPO's site (at either https://www.federalregister.gov or https://www.govinfo.gov/app/collection/FR).

---

2. 2 U.S.C. § 285b. (2012).

GPO also offers access to an unofficial copy of the *Code of Federal Regulations* that incorporates changes from the *Federal Register* as they take effect. While not official, this website, known as the Electronic *Code of Federal Regulations* or e-CFR, is extremely useful in keeping up with changes to federal regulations. This unofficial copy can be located at http://www.ecfr.gov. It is slightly less up-to-date than the online version of the *United States Code*, but at typically no more than two days out of date, it is much more current than any other version of the *Code of Federal Regulations* in any format.

In addition to providing online official copies of the *Code of Federal Regulations* and the *Federal Register*, the federal government also provides a website for tracking pending regulations. Regulations.gov (https://www.regulations.gov) allows users to read the text of both pending regulations and the text of comments that have been posted. Users can also post their own comments about proposed regulations.

b. Major Case Websites

In addition to the Kentucky sites discussed above, several other free websites offer access to case law. Some offer access to state and federal case law, while others limit their coverage to federal cases. The best known and oldest of the case law sites is FindLaw. FindLaw is currently divided into two sections, the consumer site (www.findlaw.com) and the legal professionals' site (lp.findlaw.com). For actual legal research, the legal professionals' site is much more useful than the consumer site. The legal professionals' site offers access to U.S. Supreme Court and Courts of Appeal decisions and decisions of most state supreme courts and courts of appeals. The starting date for federal court coverage varies from 1994 to 1997, depending on circuit, with coverage for most circuit courts of appeals beginning in 1995. United States Supreme Court decisions are available dating back to 1760. Coverage for Kentucky courts begins in January 1997. Starting coverage for other states varies.

The newest major, free case law website is extremely useful for its coverage of federal courts of appeals cases and federal district court cases. Justia (http://www.justia.com) offers access to Supreme Court decisions starting in 1759, and to all federal courts of appeals decisions since 1924, with selected pre-1924 opinions available for some circuits. Justia also offers free access to federal district court opinions from 1924 to the present (with selected older opinions available) and opinions from selected specialty federal courts from 1855 to the present. Moreover, Justia also offers opinions from state supreme courts and courts of appeals. Coverage for Kentucky begins in 1976 for the Supreme Court (the year the Kentucky Supreme Court was created) and December 1949 for the Kentucky Court of Appeals. Unpublished decisions are included beginning in 2002 for the Kentucky Supreme Court and in 1997 for the Kentucky Court of Appeals. Justia uses standard West print reporter citations to identify individual decisions when these citations are available. No other free service offers coverage that comes close to Justia's.

c. Briefs and Other Court Documents

There is no shortage of places to locate copies of documents filed with the federal courts. Beginning in 1988, the federal government began making court filings available electronically through a system called Public Access to Court Electronic Records, more commonly known by its acronym PACER (https://www.pacer.gov/). Estimates have put the number of court documents available on PACER in excess of 500 million[3] as of 2013. As all federal courts now require documents to be filed electronically, the number of documents available via PACER continues to grow massively each year. To access the PACER archives, a subscription is required and the PACER search interface remains stuck in the early 1990s, making it difficult to use. However, many free and commercial databases have copied documents from PACER and made these documents available through their own databases with much better searching capabilities. Large collections of federal court documents can be located on Westlaw, Lexis Advance, Bloomberg Law, Justia, Google Scholar, and several other commercial and free websites.

D. Select Search Technique

Commercial services can offer a variety of ways of searching their databases for cases, statutes, or other legal information. Usually, the larger services, such as Lexis Advance, Bloomberg Law, and Westlaw offer more than one means of searching their databases, while less expensive services offer fewer search options. As these three services are the largest and most frequently used, they are used as examples in discussing the various types of searching techniques. All three systems use a single, Google-like search box. This search box can distinguish between the most common types of searches: natural language searches, terms and connectors searches, case name searches, citation searches, or even Shepard's, KeyCite, or BCite searches. Both Westlaw and Lexis Advance

---

3. Timothy B. Lee, *The Inside Story of Aaron Swartz's Campaign to Liberate Court Filings*, arstechnica.com, http://arstechnica.com/tech-policy/2013/02/the-inside-story-of-aaron-swartzs-campaign-to-liberate-court-filings/2/ (Feb. 8, 2013).

offer a link next to an advanced searching screen next to the search box, where users can run segment searches in the citation or case name fields.

The other big change is the fact that all three systems now run searches across all their databases by default. It is no longer necessary to select a database prior to running a search. This can be both beneficial and detrimental. This new default setting ensures that a document is not missed simply because it is contained in a database other than the one being searched; however, since the search is now being run in many different databases, the results lists are much longer and it is possible that a highly relevant document may be missed simply because it is buried deeply within the results list. To combat this problem, all three services allow users to filter the results both before and after the search. Prior to performing a search, users can pre-filter the data by jurisdiction, practice area, or content type. All three systems also allow applying post-search filters. Post-search filtering can be done by keyword, practice area, jurisdiction, document type, or several other criteria. Results can also be sorted in a variety of different ways.

1. Natural Language Searching

The default search on Lexis Advance and Westlaw is "natural language" searching, while the default on Bloomberg Law is keyword searching. The default natural language search allows you to type in a simple question or phrase. The search engine will then pick out the words it thinks are important and return a list of results based on those words. Natural language searching can be beneficial to new legal researchers, but it does lack the precision of terms and connectors searching, discussed below. Natural language search engines are designed to produce a list of results and rank the results in the order that the search engine determines is the most relevant.

A few caveats about natural language searching are important. The first is that the search engine is ranking the results by its own predetermined criteria, which may or may not be the criteria that are important to the person conducting the research. Second, the natural language search engines are designed to return a minimum number of results whether or not those documents are really relevant to the search terms that have been used. This can produce a substantial number of false hits.

2. Terms and Connectors Searching

All legal databases make use of some form of terms and connectors search, although the connectors used may vary. In Westlaw and Lexis Advance, a terms

Figure 11-1. Illustration of Boolean Connectors

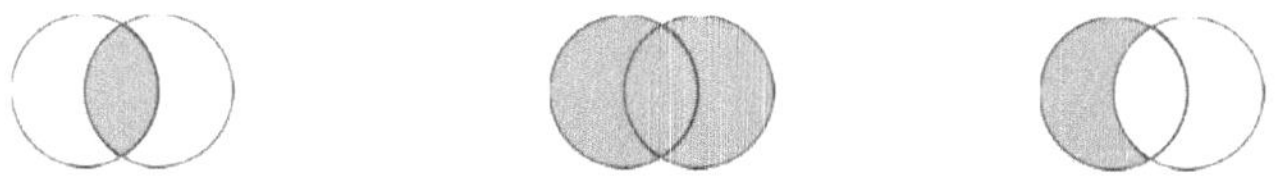

Automobile AND Accident Ship OR Boat Engineers NOT Railroad

and connectors search can be run from either the main search bar or from the advanced search screen. The advanced search screens may be more useful because they list the different connectors available on each system. Bloomberg Law does not yet offer an advanced search screen. In terms and connectors searching, several different concepts can be used together to refine searches so that only the most relevant documents are returned. Terms and connectors searching employs the use of connectors, wildcards, and nesting in order to generate effective searches. While natural language searching uses artificial intelligence to rank the documents, terms and connectors searches rank the documents by how often the search words appear in the document. This gives the researcher much more power to customize their searches.

Connectors determine where search terms will appear in a document relative to one another. Effective use of connectors is critical in locating relevant authority. Connectors come in two forms: basic connectors and proximity connectors.

a. Basic Boolean Connectors

In terms and connectors searching using basic Boolean search connectors, the connectors are nothing more than conjunctions: "and," "or," "but not." "And" is a restrictive connector, in that both terms must be present for the document to be retrieved. Thus, in a search for **"automobile AND accident"** both the term "automobile" and the term "accident" must be within the document. "Or" is often used when a search strategy includes synonyms. Either term in the search may be present in the retrieved documents. Thus, a search for **"ship OR boat"** will retrieve documents including either term. "But not" (often expressed in searches as not) is used to exclude specified terms. A search for **"engineers NOT railroad"** might retrieve cases involving civil or electrical engineers, but not those driving trains (see Figure 11-1). Quotation marks can also be used to make the system search for an exact phrase.

b. Proximity Connectors

While the basic connectors can be useful, proximity connectors can return documents with much more relevance. Proximity connectors tell the computer to search for documents in which the search terms appear within a certain distance of each other. Lexis Advance, Westlaw, and Bloomberg Law all make use of proximity connectors (as do many other case law databases), although the format used varies slightly between the three services. Lexis uses "w/s" and "w/p" to indicate that the search terms should appear within the same sentence or same paragraph, respectively. Westlaw uses the predefined proximity connectors "/s" and "/p" as its predefined terms, while Bloomberg law uses "S/" and "P/." Additionally, all three services allow researchers to specify different distances between search terms by replacing the "s" or the "p" with a number. For example, using "w/5" on Lexis or "/5" on Westlaw would require that the search terms appear within five words of each other. There are variations on these searches. Using a plus sign in front of the connector (i.e. +5, +s, +p) on Westlaw requires that the first word appear before the second word in addition to being within five words, the same sentence, or same paragraph. The same function can be accomplished on Lexis Advance by using "pre/" followed by a number and on Bloomberg Law by using "N/5." Lexis Advance has no specific equivalent for +s or +p, but the same result can be obtained by using a number that approximates the number of words in a sentence or paragraph (For example, fifteen words for a sentence and 50 words for a paragraph). Bloomberg uses "NP/*x*" (with x being a number) to find words that appear in a specific order and within *x* words of each other.

c. Wildcards and Truncators

Two forms of wildcards are typically used in Boolean searching. First, all three of the major services use an exclamation point as a root expander (also known as a truncator). A root expander finds all words that begin with the letters prior to the exclamation point. It can only be used at the end of a series of letters. For example, **"employ!"** would find all words that begin with the word employ, such as *employee, employed, employer, employment*, etc. Take care in placing a root expander, however, or you may obtain bizarre results. Using the search **"emp!"** would find not only employ and related words, but also such words as *empathy, empty, emphasis, empanelled*, etc.

The other form of wildcard serves as a placeholder and can be used anywhere in a word. Westlaw and Bloomberg Law use the asterisk (*) as the standard symbol for a placeholder, while Lexis Advance uses a question mark (?). Typically, use placeholders when you are unsure about the spelling of a word or unsure which form of a word is used. For example, searching for "**dr*nk**," would find *drink*, *drank*, and *drunk*. Usually, up to three placeholders can be used in a single word when conducting a search. In certain instances, the placeholder may be preferable to the root expander at the end of a word. Using an expander on "**trad!**" with hopes of finding *trade*, *trading*, *trades*, etc., will also produce results that include *traditional*.

d. Segment and Field Searching

Another way of restricting the number of documents returned by a terms and connectors search is to limit the locations in which the search terms can be found to certain portions of the document. Lexis and Westlaw both allow researchers to limit searches in several ways, such as by date, name, or citation, in most of their databases. In case law databases, restrictions can be placed on the sections of the document in which the search terms appear. Lexis calls these sections "segments" while Westlaw calls them "fields." Bloomberg Law does not appear to allow this type of searching, although it does allow post-search filtering.

e. Combining Search Strategies

By combining these search strategies, a researcher can create a complex search strategy designed to retrieve cases that are extremely relevant to the search subject. For example, to find recent court decisions concerning the liability of parents whose minor children used their computer to download music from file sharing services, you might try a search strategy similar to this: **DA(> 2010) AND (infring! /s copyright) /p (Internet OR web OR online) AND "liability of parent for minor child."**

In this example, the date field "**DA(>2010)**" search instructs the system that any case retrieved must be newer than the year 2010. Truncating the root "**infring**" means that a document containing any form of the words *infringed*, *infringing* and *infringe* will be retrieved, but only if it appears in the same sentence as copyright. The parentheses around *Internet*, *web*, and *online* groups them and instructs the system to perform the "or" functions before applying the proximity connector "/p" or the "and" connectors. The last portion requires the phrase "liability of parent for minor child" to also appear somewhere in the document. Combining multiple search techniques together using parentheses is called *nesting*.

E. Review and Refine the Search

Often, your first search will not produce the best results. By reviewing the results and refining the search, you can find more relevant documents. For instance, an initial search using terms and connectors might yield 1,000 results (or more) or no results. The key to finding good information is practice. With practice comes the ability to craft more precise searches that will produce more relevant results.

Some basic strategies can be used to enhance the effectiveness of a terms and connectors search. If a search produces no results, you might need broader connectors such as searching for terms in the same paragraph instead of the same sentence. Other strategies for broadening searches that return no results are including synonyms for the search terms used or searching a larger database. For searches that produce too many results, the solutions are exactly the opposite. Using narrower connectors (e.g., looking for terms in the same sentence instead of the same paragraph), using narrower search terms, and searching smaller databases are all ways of reducing the number of results.

Do not assume that searches which return a large number of results are always bad. In some instances, it may be a good strategy to actually construct a broad search and narrow it using the tools provided by the services. As mentioned earlier, post-search filtering can be done using a variety of filters. In addition, Westlaw and Lexis Advance offer the ability to narrow a search by using the "Search Within Results" search box to add additional terms, while in Bloomberg Law the same result can be accomplished by adding additional terms to the search box.

Appendix A

Citation

I. General Legal Citation

There are two legal citation manuals used by American lawyers. The oldest, and most widely used, is *The Bluebook: A Uniform System of Citation*, now in its twentieth edition. Used for decades in law reviews, it is the most likely guide to be found in a law firm. The other citation manual is the *ALWD Guide to Legal Citation*, 5th ed., which is still primarily only used in law schools. As both are somewhat expensive and rather detailed for everyday use, a thrifty researcher might want to purchase Charles Lipson's *Cite Right: A Quick Guide to Citation Style—MLA, APA, Chicago, the Sciences, Professions, and More* (2006), which has chapters on both the *Bluebook* and *AWLD* styles.

Both *Bluebook* and *AWLD* are very similar in most regards. In general, most case law citations conform to a common pattern, while statutes, regulations, and secondary sources vary widely among jurisdictions and by formats.

A basic case citation begins with an abbreviated version of the party names, either underlined or in italics. This information is followed by a comma, then the volume number of the reporter in which the case is found, the recognized abbreviation of the case reporter, and the page number where the case begins. After this, there is a parenthetical with an abbreviation for the jurisdiction deciding the case and the year when the case was decided. For example:

> *Case name [party v. party]*, volume number / reporter abbreviation / page number (jurisdiction / year)

> *Acme v. Coyote*, 566 S.W.3d 123 (Ky. 2001)

A few other simple citation forms can be found in Table A-1.

Table A-1. Sample Citation Forms

Statutes	17 U.S.C. § 107 (2006)
Regulations	16 C.F.R. § 319 (2011)
Cases	*Steelvest, Inc. v. Scansteel Serv. Ctr., Inc.*, 807 S.W.2d 476 (Ky. 1991)
	Roe v. Wade, 410 U.S. 113 (1973)
	Kendrick v. Bland, 541 F. Supp. 21 (W.D. Ky. 1981)
Federal Rules	FRE 802 (Federal Rules of Evidence)

II. Kentucky Legal Citation

In many contexts, Kentucky lawyers use the citation forms found in the *Bluebook* or the *ALWD Guide*. However, in some cases, Kentucky court rules and state statutes mandate a certain citation form. For example, Kentucky Rule of Civil Procedure CR 76.12(4)(g) requires that the Kentucky Revised Statutes be cited as "KRS," as in KRS 507.020, as opposed to the *Bluebook*'s Ky. Rev. Stat. Ann. § 507.020. In another example, the Kentucky legislature, in KRS 13A.222(4)(l)(2), prescribes the format for citations to new session laws published in the *Kentucky Acts*, using a format that has been long used in Kentucky, but one that does not resemble *Bluebook* or *ALWD* format (see Table A-2). Some Kentucky sources instruct researchers in citation. For instance, the Kentucky Administrative Regulations has a "How to Cite" guide in its front matter.

When preparing documents for Kentucky courts, it is always important to follow these local variations. For more detail on statutory and customary ci-

Table A-2. Kentucky Citation Forms

Statutes	KRS 507.020 (Kentucky Revised Statutes)
Session Law	2011 Ky. Acts ch. 168, sec. 2 (*Kentucky Acts*)
Regulations	108 KAR 25:100 (*Kentucky Administrative Regulations Service*)
	29 Ky. R. 25 (*Administrative Register of Kentucky*)
Cases	*Steelvest, Inc. v. Scansteel Service Center, Inc.*, 807 S.W.2d 476 (Ky. 1991)
Court Rules	CR 41.02 (Kentucky Rules of Civil Procedure)
	RCr 5.02 (Kentucky Rules of Criminal Procedure)

tation practices in Kentucky, see Kurt X. Metzmeier and Leah R. Smith, "Citation of Kentucky Legal Materials" in Kurt X. Metzmeier et al., *Kentucky Legal Research Manual,* (4th ed., Office of Continuing Legal Education, University of Kentucky College of Law 2016).

Appendix B

Selected Bibliography

General Research

Steven Barkan, Barbara Bintliff & Mary Whisner, *Fundamentals of Legal Research* (10th ed., Foundation Press 2015).

Robert C. Berring & Elizabeth A. Edinger, *Finding the Law* (12th ed., West 2005).

Morris L. Cohen & Kent C. Olson, *Legal Research in a Nutshell* (12th ed., West 2016).

Amy E. Sloan, *Basic Legal Research* (6th ed., Wolters Kluwer 2015).

Kentucky Research

Helene Davis, "Kentucky Practice Materials: A Selected Annotated Bibliography," in *State Practice Materials: Annotated Bibliographies* (Frank G. Houdek, ed., W.S. Hein 2005).

Kurt X. Metzmeier, et al., *Kentucky Legal Research Manual* (4th ed., Office of Continuing Legal Education, University of Kentucky College of Law 2016).

Advanced Legal Research

J.D.S. Armstrong & Christopher A. Knott, *Where the Law Is: An Introduction to Advanced Legal Research* (4th ed., Thomson/West 2013).

Leah F. Chanin, Penny A. Hazelton & Joseph J. Beard, *Specialized Legal Research* (Aspen 2014).

Roby B. Sawyers, William A. Raabe, Gerald E. Whittenburg & Steven L. Gill, *Federal Tax Research* (10th ed., Cengage 2015).

Legal Analysis

Bryan A Garner, *The Redbook: A Manual on Legal Style* (3d ed., Thomson/West 2013).

Laurel Currie Oates & Anne Enquist, *The Legal Writing Handbook* (6th ed., Wolters Kluwer Law & Business 2014).

Mary Barnard Ray & Jill J. Ramsfield, *Legal Writing: Getting It Right and Getting It Written* (5th ed., Thomson/West 2010).

Mary Barnard Ray, *The Basics of Legal Writing* (rev. 1st ed., Thomson/West 2008).

Helene S. Shapo, Marilyn R. Walter & Elizabeth Fajans, *Writing and Analysis in the Law* (6th ed., Foundation Press 2013).

About the Authors

William A. Hilyerd is an associate professor of legal bibliography at the University of Louisville's Louis D. Brandeis School of Law. He teaches advanced legal research. He is currently working on the third edition of *Reversible Error in Kentucky Criminal Cases*. He contributed the chapters on administrative law, court rules and ethics, citators, and online research.

Kurt X. Metzmeier is the associate director of the University of Louisville's Louis D. Brandeis School of Law Library and a professor of legal bibliography. He recently completed a history of Kentucky's pioneer law reporters, *Writing the Legal Record: Law Reporters in Nineteenth-Century Kentucky*. He wrote the chapters on constitutional law, statutory law, legislative history, and secondary sources research.

David Ensign is the director of the Law Library at the Louis D. Brandeis School of Law, University of Louisville. He also teaches and writes about copyright law. He was responsible for chapters on the research process, analysis, and judicial opinions.

Index